GRIEG

GRIEG

GRIEG

A SYMPOSIUM

Edited by

GERALD ABRAHAM

UNIVERSITY OF OKLAHOMA PRESS
NORMAN

First published in England by Lindsay Drummond Limited, 1948

First American edition published by the University of
Oklahoma Press, 1950. All rights reserved

Printed in Great Britain

Contents

Preface

GRIEG, in the opinion of Superior Persons, is something less than one of the great masters in music. Was he, in fact, with his narrow range, his limited fertility, and his defective technique, a ' master ' in any sense of the word? He was certainly a master of the song. But in other respects? No one would claim that he is one of the world's greatest composers but he is, I think, a genuine minor master and, as Mr. Horton says in his chapter on Grieg's style, ' the world of music owes a debt to the minority of executants, critics and amateurs who make it their business to call our attention to the claims of the *petits maîtres,* inciting us to enquire not only into the defects that keep them *petits* but also into the virtues that make them *maîtres.*' Moreover genuine, searching musical criticism—as distinguished from the clever play of words and thoughts over the surface of music, and from mere formal and thematic analysis—can give fresh interest to the most hackneyed music.

We are often, even the Superior Persons, shockingly ignorant about a great deal of this ' hackneyed music '. There are, for instance, few more familiar compositions in the whole repertory than the Grieg Piano Concerto. Yet most of us listen to it in partial ignorance, believing we are hearing something Grieg wrote in his twenties, in 1868, whereas a great many of the sounds that come to us from the orchestra are sounds conceived by Grieg at the very end of his life. And quite a lot of Grieg—as it happens, some of the very best of Grieg—is not hackneyed at all. Every schoolgirl knows the Grieg who approximates to Chaminade; many a professional musician is ignorant of the Grieg who approximates to Bartók.

Grieg's music is open to criticism on many counts, but it cannot be passed over as unworthy of study by anyone who loves or admires the work of the greater men who came under his spell. Take Debussy, for instance. Debussy's true attitude to Grieg is most certainly not stated in that often quoted epigram about a ' pink bon-bon stuffed with snow ' nor in his anti-Dreyfusard description of Grieg in 1903 as ' like a genial photographer '. One of Debussy's earliest musical memories was of a Norwegian carpenter in Cannes ' qui chantait du matin au soir—peut-être du Grieg ', and as late as 1914 he played the piano part in a public performance of a Grieg violin sonata. Grieg perhaps had a more important share in the formation of Debussy's style than we have generally supposed. It is a commonplace that Debussy's String Quartet owes something to Borodin; hardly anyone has observed that it owes considerably more to Grieg, specifically to one of Grieg's weaker works, the G minor Quartet. True, there is no obvious Griegishness in the Debussy Quartet, but the most casual study of the parallels between Grieg's G minor Quartet of 1878 and Debussy's G minor Quartet of 1893 shows that the one was modelled to some extent on the other, or at least that it was written with the other in the composer's conscious or sub-conscious mind. (Do composers work in that way? Yes. For have we not Sabaneev's description of Skryabin's writing-table at the time when he was working on *Prometheus*, with the scores of *Heldenleben, La Mer*, and Glazunov's Sixth Symphony ' which obviously served him as guides in orchestration '?) Not only are both quartets evolved almost entirely from a motto-theme: both motto-themes begin with the same four notes. Even the semiquaver triplet in Debussy has its parallel in the melody of Grieg's second movement. After the enunciation of the motto-theme, both quartets break into quicker movement, pianissimo— and Grieg's quaver figure is echoed in the très mouvementé section of Debussy's finale. Both first movements end with rapid passages in which the motto-theme, broken into repeated quav   ,..ayed by all four instruments in octaves. Both finales begin with the motto-theme in slowish duple time, then break into a quicker tempo in 6/8 or 12/8; both end in the tonic major, presto or très vif, with a big crescendo at the end—and the très vif metamorphosis of Debussy's motto-theme is closely related to Grieg's saltarello. Finally consider the scoring, the quartet texture; take the Peters-Eulenburg miniature score of the Grieg and the Durand miniature score of the Debussy and compare p. 5 of Grieg with p. 6 of Debussy, p. 6 with p. 7, pp. 7 and 25 with p. 48, and 70 with 42.

Grieg's music, then, is worth studying; at any rate Debussy found it so. In the following pages it is studied more thoroughly than ever before, at least more thoroughly than ever before in English. And the list of works is, I believe, the fullest and most accurate yet published in any language, though two of the most important parts of it— the lists of Grieg's songs and piano music compiled by Miss Astra Desmond and Mrs. Kathleen Dale—have already appeared, in rather different forms, in *Music and Letters*. I am indebted to the editor of that invaluable quarterly for permission to reprint both the lists and revised and considerably extended forms of the critical studies to which they were appended.

My grateful thanks are also due to my friend Mr. Gerik Schjelderup, son of one of Grieg's first biographers, for reading the proofs and guiding me through the tangle of Norwegian spelling.

G.A.

1

Grieg the Man

By

Gerik Schjelderup

WHAT WAS GRIEG LIKE as a man? The artist gives the answer in his work. And in music the man in the artist reveals himself more clearly than in any other form of art. The more we understand music the better will we be able to form through his music a picture of the composer as a person. Still our curiosity is not always satisfied or at least we like to make sure that we were right in our impressions of the man as we see him in his music.

So first of all: What did Grieg look like? My father, the Norwegian composer Gerhard Schjelderup, sixteen years Grieg's junior, knew him well and received many delightful letters from him. In his Grieg biography we find the following description :

> Grieg was of small stature, delicate but impressive. The fine serene forehead he had in common with many a creative artist. His light blue eyes under the bushy eyebrows sparkled like those of a child when listening to a fairy tale. They mostly had a joyful though gentle and dreaming expression, but when roused to sudden anger or indignation they could flash like lightning. For with his short stumpy nose, the fine flowing hair, the firm expressive mouth under the strong moustache, and the resolute chin, he had dynamic energy and an impatient and passionate temperament. As in Wagner's features there was in his a marked contrast between the upper and lower parts of the face. The forehead reveals the dreamer, the mouth and chin a strong determination to live a life of untiring activity. Grieg's astounding energy gave to his frail body an elastic and impressive gait and more than once in his life he performed true feats of endurance.

What strikes one most about Grieg as a man is his depth and warmth of feeling, his disarming sense of humour, and childlike appreciation of the ridiculous, but also a great simplicity and clearness of thought and above all an amazing modesty and lack of conceit. In all his struggles with ill-health and the many adversities that confront most creative artists in a material world, he always retained the child's capacity for enjoyment.

It was loyalty which forced Alexander Greig of Aberdeen,

stubbornly faithful to the cause of the Stuarts, to emigrate to Norway after Culloden, to which fact we owe the very existence of his great-grandson as a Norwegian composer; and this same loyalty is a strong characteristic also of Grieg himself. Ever faithful in his affections he gave throughout his life many proofs of friendship and sympathy for his fellow artists. Not since Liszt had any composer shown such active interest in the struggles of his younger colleagues when he himself had become world-famous. The following letter is typical of this warm sympathy :

> Many thanks for your charming youthful letter from which I conclude that you are far from turning into a philistine. I know you'd rather lose nose, mouth and ears than do that. I agree that we live in a time which is poor in art, but as we get older we should try to appreciate the best that the youth of to-day can offer. We must not live only in the ideals of our own youth. It's nonsense to talk so much about being faithful to the ideals of one's youth. There is room for development surely. I have always felt happiest in life when I thought I had added if only a little to the ideals of my youth. What is life more than a struggle for the realisation of truths? How could one stop at the ideals of one's confirmation age? To-day I love Schumann, but in a different way to when I was seventeen, and I love Wagner but differently from when I was twenty-seven. So one's love for music like one's love for a woman changes its character as time passes and it is not less beautiful for that but rather improves as wine does. Don't worry if you can't feel in the same way as when you were seventeen as long as your feelings are true and sincere.

Grieg was always happiest when he could work and fight for the cause of music and not only for his own music but even more for that of others. Thus he considered it a great achievement in his life when he was the first to arrange a concert programme consisting exclusively of Norwegian music and when later in 1898 he organised a National Musical Festival in Bergen, where every young Norwegian composer of promise was given a hearing.

On the first of these occasions the attendance of the public was lamentably small but when afterwards the six concerts given at Bergen were each attended by three thousand people, Grieg was triumphant indeed. He was the sponsor and actual organiser of these concerts. In the face of narrow-minded local patriotism he insisted that one of the very finest European orchestras should be engaged. He would have no half-measures. It had to be the famous Dutch Concertgebouw Orchestra under Mengelberg. The result was an unqualified success in every respect and Grieg expressed his joy and satisfaction in glowing terms in a number of letters.

In all his later personal triumphs both in his own country and in the capitals of Europe he always showed cool judgment. Although he could be thrilled and excited, he was always ready to add some humorous touches in his comments. When at the age of forty his fame had spread to England he was received by Queen Victoria at Windsor Castle. After the visit he writes : ' The Queen is charming and certainly *most* intelligent. For were not her first words to me : " I am a great admirer of your compositions." ' And from Holland he writes :

> I am so popular here that people come up to me in the streets and ask : ' Have I the honour of talking to Mr. Grieg? ' . . . At the concert two Queens were present. They conveyed to me their thanks and greetings and that I should be made Knight of the Order of Orange-Nassau. If you know me rightly you will understand how happy this made me as orders and medals are most useful to me in the top layer of my trunks. The Customs officials are always so kind to me at the sight of them.

Throughout his life Grieg retained a childlike simplicity and a capacity to be enchanted by the beauties of nature or art or by joyful events, and he could express his feelings in a most appealing way. When in his latter years ill-health made it more difficult for him to work he remarks : ' When Pegasus refuses to run he is more obstinate than a Roman donkey, the more you beat him the more stubbornly he stays put. And as I am a member of the N.S.P.C.A. I feel obliged to spare the poor beast a little.'

Of the great composers of the world he spoke with the deepest respect and admiration and of himself most modestly. ' Artists like Bach and Beethoven,' he told a German interviewer, ' erected churches and temples on ethereal heights. My aim in my music is exactly what Ibsen says about his own plays: "I want to build homes for the people in which they can be happy and contented ".' As a critic Grieg was appreciative of many varied composers; he often took to the pen in defence of one whom he thought had been unjustly attacked and he could be quite merciless in his counter-strokes. He hated fashions and cliques and ridiculed them more than once. When fanatical followers of Wagner attacked Schumann or Mozart or Brahms, Grieg would make biting comments in essays published in the English and German musical Press.

As a thinker Grieg was not inclined to philosophical ponderings. He was in fact convinced that philosophy, the art of reasoning, was adverse, and therefore harmful, to the imaginative art of music. It strikes one almost as a contradiction of this when in his views on religion he seems to employ rather more reason than imagination. In a letter written from hospital only a few days before his death in 1907 he writes:

> ... To be able to talk about matters regarding my religious views would need a better state of health than the one I am in at present. So let this suffice: During a visit to England in 1888 I was much taken by the teachings of the Unitarians who believe in one God alone, to the exclusion of the Holy Trinity in which God the Son is equal to God the Father. This conception was most acceptable to me then and during the past eighteen years I have not come to any better conclusions. Although people have tried to persuade me of something else, it has carried no conviction with me. As for science—that is all very well as a means to an end but, oh—to what end? It seems a very unsatisfactory one to me. I firmly believe in the existence of God, but I find it hard to accept the idea of a personal prayer to the deity.

Although Grieg's strong sense of liberty and individual outlook would not allow him to accept any rigid doctrines or conventions his nature was deeply religious, as one would expect from any poetic mind, and in those of his works that are based on a religious theme we find a deep sincere devoutness. His great love of nature and admiration of its wonders gave his conceptions a strongly pantheistic character.

Outwardly Grieg's life seemed blessed with early success. At a comparatively early age he found his own artistic personality and gained world recognition. But in his work are distinct traces of the struggles that took place within him. His essentially lyrical temperament made him subject to many and varying moods but his strong will allowed him to control them with a firm hand when he had to take important decisions. He was always keenly interested in political and social conditions but was wise enough not to let himself be involved in matters alien to him as an artist. It was certainly not indifference with him, because he followed the fate of his country and that of humanity in general with deep compassion. In his sympathies he was a true democrat, indeed a republican. He confessed a love for the people, but it was not an uncritical one. He visualised a more ideal people of the future, much changed and led by an aristocracy of the spirit. In a letter to his German publisher, Dr. Abraham, he says:

> I wish you could read an article by Kropotkin in which he wishes among other things the following: Need we wonder that when the upper classes have no scruples in butchering thousands or even hundreds of thousands of workers and peasants, that the lower classes

barred from all education want to reverse things and say: ' What do I care if I kill every member of the upper classes if it will make them think and bring about more tolerable conditions for everybody.' Both sides are wrong of course. We must start with education but above all we must stop mass slaughter authorised from above.

And Grieg adds : ' Do you think these are Utopian ideals? Believe me—there will be other times; they will come whether through blood or intelligence. Let us hope through the latter! ' In his conclusion Grieg shows his warm sympathy for a suffering and tortured humanity and a conviction that only through our own continuous efforts can we hope to make a better world.

As I have said earlier, Grieg could be very sociable at times and thoroughly enjoy festivities and his own public appearances—he was a very impressive and amusing impromptu after-dinner speaker— but all the same he was essentially a lonely, unworldly figure, who hardly ever revealed himself in words, not even to his nearest and dearest. The few who knew him intimately agreed that he was a proud and noble nature. Like any other mortal he would err, but he was the first to admit it and he would do so with a disarming frankness. He was his own strictest critic.

2

The Orchestral Music

By

Hubert Foss

'THE THOUGHT OF A PIECE in six movements,' wrote Grieg to his friend Julius Röntgen,[1] 'fills me with sorrow and envy.' The composer explained and excused the feeling on the grounds of ill-health : and, indeed, pathologically it may well be that he suffered from a lack of continuing creative energy which affected him psychologically. The musical facts remain. For whatever reason, however analytically expounded, Grieg found, after his friendship with Nordraak, the whole German process of musical composition distasteful to him in a high degree. He disliked, rather than was incapable of, the elaborate system of musical development, the flowing musical texture woven introvertly by the Romantic musical brain. His instinct told him to harness the waterfall of ideas into a narrower, more manageable—almost more domestic—channel than the spouting seas of Liszt and Wagner. Never touched in his manhood by the *kolossal*, Grieg was determined, content, to be a small master : his deliberate smallness is one of his greatest virtues.

In truth, Grieg was as personal in his handling of the orchestra as he was in the shaping of his fundamental musical phrases. His three deep loves were almost equal in their strength : love for his country and its folk-music, for the violin (so apt for the national dance), and for the piano. But though he had a good technique in scoring and a fine personal, critical estimate of sound, it is certain that Grieg did not compose orchestrally : that is to say, he did not write mentally into the orchestra. He conceived his music in terms of the piano or the voice and after that translated the ideas into orchestral colour and development. That, it would seem, explains why the most important of his instrumental works (the theatre music is critically dealt with in another chapter) is the Piano Concerto. His ideas were drawn out by, and followed the lead of, his own beloved instrument, around which he could array his decorative orchestral colourings.

[1] Röntgen: *Grieg* (s' Gravenhage, 1930). Letter of May 31, 1892.

In this work the texture is mainly continued by the solo instrument : there is, indeed, hardly a moment of purely orchestral musical conception. The strongly personal idiom, so reduced to bare piano terms as it was, would fit easily into orchestral dress, and would make a music Grieg himself liked to hear. It is not surprising how few, and how obvious, are the changes he made in re-costuming the songs and pieces which he transcribed for the larger body of players. Removing himself from the necessity to conceive music in an orchestral medium when he arranged, or when the theatre gave him a lead of subject, Grieg could do far better with the orchestra than at other moments : so he used it but little for his daily round of musical thought.

Apart from the *Norwegian Dances* orchestrated by Hans Sitt (originally written for piano duet, Op. 35) and the *Lyric Suite*, which the composer edited and altered from Anton Seidl's arrangement for orchestra of four piano pieces from Op. 54, and of course the theatre pieces and suites therefrom, the orchestral output is small : the Piano Concerto, Op. 16, the overture *I Höst* (*In Autumn*) Op. 11, *Old Norwegian Melody with Variations*, Op. 51, the *Symphonic Dances*, Op. 64; the curious melodrama *Bergljot*, orchestrated many years after its first writing-down; for strings only, the *Holberg Suite*, Op. 40, originally written for piano, *Two Elegiac Melodies*, Op. 34, *Two Norwegian Tunes*, Op. 63, arrangements of two of the *Lyric Pieces*, Op. 68, for strings, or strings, oboe and horn, and of two of the songs, Op. 53, and one song *Den Bergtekne*, Op. 32, for voice, strings and two horns.

The composer's individual outlook on the orchestra is well shown by the Seidl incident. Grieg did not see Seidl's version of the four piano pieces until after the conductor's death and wrote[1] that there was ' much that is excellent in it. Here and there my intentions have not been carried out, and my question now is, will the widow allow me to make the changes called for? Without them I cannot send the pieces to Peters, but with them I shall be glad to do so.' In a second letter he wrote : ' Seidl's orchestration was undeniably very good from his point of view, but was too heavy (*dick*) for my intentions. The whole Wagnerian apparatus was used for my mood pictures which did not suit me in all cases.' It would appear to be impossible to-day (at least without unattainable journeys) to compare Grieg's revision of the score with that which Seidl performed in New York. Grieg's is undoubtedly brilliantly successful; but how

[1] H. T. Finck's translation.

much is Seidl and how much Grieg cannot be more than guessed. The printed score is certainly heavier, still, than his normal style.

Grieg did not, we are told, dislike Wagner's music. But it is certain that he shrank into his house above Bergen at the thought of the Wagnerian business, the way of life, the conscription of all the arts into the service of one Germanic and gigantic impressionism. At once uncertain of himself (look at his apology for the fate of his pieces in ' third-class hotels ') and firm in his artistic search for a small perfection, every work to be an absolute and completely finished thing, he developed a separate orchestral manner. From that water-surrounded villa, he looked out across the hills and the years, and saw Schubert rather than Berlioz. He looked less and less south-eastwards to Leipzig and Weimar. He had no illusions about the size of his ideas; and he scored them perfectly to scale in his manhood. In the *Autumn* overture we find a marked interest in primary colours, rather than a blend of shades always mixing into one another. The opening movement of the *Peer Gynt* Suite, No. 1—*Morning Mood*—is so familiar that one either hears it mangled by a café band or is inclined to avoid it in the real life of the Henry Wood Promenade Concerts (for example). To listen to it as Grieg wrote it for orchestra is a refreshing experience : it also gives a key to his methods with the orchestra. It would perhaps be opportune here to discuss those methods.

Essentially a melodist, but not a contrapuntist, Grieg had an acute sense of harmony as an emotional element in music. It follows that with the orchestra, he would be more interested in melodic outlines than in general texture. In the orchestral works, despite a good deal of careful ingenuity, there is very little creative work in the part-weaving : as in the piano works, every detail is subordinated to the two main objects of presenting first melody and secondly moving harmony. Even in the transcriptions of piano pieces, in which the folk-like repetitions of short phrases are a (sometimes criticised) characteristic, the composer does not as a rule alter his colouring for the repeat. Nor does he cross phrases with different instrumental interjections. The claims of each instrument are not inventively met. The result is that no composer has ever orchestrated less in the way of musical thinking of (shall we say?) Berlioz, Liszt, Wagner, Florent Schmitt, Elgar or Bax.

Rhythmically, Grieg's music is not complicated, its melody does not depend upon inner cross-rhythms. This point again restricts the texture, for the composer liked clarity first of all. Trills, tremolandos, counter-melodies, rhythmic interjections, and the common orchestral tricks, are scarce. The whole music is as lucid as a brilliant painting made for children, and as engaging. Three other points are worth adding to this paragraph, flowing from the argument before exposed. The first is a part, too, of the folk-song-and-dance tradition, a noticeable persistence of pedal, or at least too static, basses. The second is the comparative rarity of the occasions a melodic line is doubled by a secondary instrument at the unison : often, on the other hand, at the octave, a device which gives a more individual colouring and a stronger carrying-power. The third point is the persistently marked contrast of family with family, as against the prevailing nineteenth-century habit of mingling the sounds of the various groups. It is a deliberate aiming at high, bright colours, at the target of simplicity. Grieg's scoring is not as direct nor as simple as Schubert's, but it is more individual. In the string department, it is far more elaborate, of course, and a much greater pleasure-seeking element—for was not Grieg a delighter in beautiful sound, a lover of line and colour before form?

The youthful overture, *In Autumn*, can be quickly disposed of as a complete work of art. It stands at a turning-point; the youthful composer had not had the years to throw off his student influences, to find his own manner, to shed conventional tricks and absorb into himself the true teaching of the academics. The work is gusty and buoyant but not very individual; a hundred other works for large orchestra must have been produced in the same decade of equal achievement if not of equal promise. But the actual orchestration reminds us that the whole thing was completely rescored more than twenty years later, in 1887. However, there are interesting points about *In Autumn* which make one look a little closer. It was written in Rome in 1866 and is designated as Op. 11. But its thematic basis is the song *Efteraarsstormen* (The Autumn Storm), Op. 18, No. 4, composed the year before. A comparison of the opening of the song with the statement of the same phrase in the orchestra is illuminating. The song opens as in Ex. 1 (see end of book); it continues by a major statement of the first idea (modified) which is a little Schubertian; that is, of course, in F major. After a climax we get an allegro molto vivace with a new idea, also a little Schubertian, in D major—a not distinguished but thoroughly energetic melody. We turn to the *Autumn* overture and find the same tune as that which informs the song, in a new orchestral dress (Ex. 2). The comparison is worth making in an immediate showing. Observe the slightly different harmony in bars 2–3 of Ex. 2 as compared with bars 1–2 of Ex. 1. The agitato phrases of descending semitones are particularly interesting. In the overture Grieg uses a phrase which is threefold in significance : it could come into more or less any of his pieces, had he chosen it; it is national; and it is full of meaning. I quote the phrase in short (Ex. 3) as it appears at the opening of the piece, with its characteristic fall of the leading note.

So much for the introduction to the song-figure. The question is, how does Grieg end the work—for the rhythmic figure of *Efteraars-stormen* is an obvious thesis for quick argument and interplay of ideas among the orchestral families? They can quarrel amicably, and agree with rancour just as they wish. Grieg refuses to take the bait of his heroic song-ending. He prefers another idea altogether, a harvesters' song, a noble tune (Ex. 4). It is in many ways a fine and original work, this overture. Yet it has the Leipzig touch imprinted on it.

The Piano Concerto, on the other hand, with its opus number standing only five figures farther down the list, opens up new ground, very fertile soil at that. The simplicity of method is quite astonishing for one who had had little experience with the orchestra since his student days. Grieg was not well known when the score was published in 1872 : he was then twenty-nine years of age. To-day the work is so successful that everyone assumes he knows it. But a study of the original score published by Fritzsch, to which my remarks generally refer,[1] reveals an originality uncommon at that period. The demand is for only two horns (in E) and at the same time for three trombones and tuba. The scoring is so light as to be almost primitive —alternating families, the upper strings kept in the lower octaves, close among themselves. The doubling is interesting, e.g. in the repeat of the first subject the first violins and bassoons double in octaves in the last bar (Ex. 5)—the bassoons were afterwards taken out—and the basses come in alone a little later, in the second subject. The rests are admirably placed. In the third movement, nine bars after A (pp. 69–70 of the Eulenberg miniature score) the solo bassoon has a little phrase crossing the bar line, a touch (preserved in the final version) that many more experienced scorers would not have thought of. There is a pleasant passage for solo 'cello with piano later (beginning on p. 83 of the miniature score) : an almost Bach-like idea. And still the strings keep in the low register. The tuttis are loud and

---

[1] The differences between the original score and the definitive form with which we are all familiar are discussed in the next chapter.

sometimes splendid, but they are sudden, not built up in layers of sound; they lack the overpowering richness of the other composers of Grieg's day. Throughout the Piano Concerto there persists a great coolness; air blows through the pages of print, and the high emotion is never blurred by heat of stoves or adorers' breath. It is precise in intention, superb in achievement. Only one other piece in the category comes alongside it : the *Holberg* Suite for strings alone.

The *Symphonic Dances*, Op. 64, make perhaps Grieg's largest-scale offering to the orchestral world, just as the Ballade in G minor, Op. 24, is (apart from the Piano Sonata, Op. 7) his most extended work for solo piano, and, like the Ballade, they are all based on Norwegian folk-tunes : Nos. 1 and 2 on hallings, No. 3 on a springdans from Amot, No. 4 on the song *Såg du nokke kjaeringa mi* and a wedding tune from Valders. The work is planned on a big scale : it comes in the list immediately after the *Two Norwegian Tunes*. For one person at least this is, on the other hand, not equal in size and musical value. For all its energy, its elaborate lay-out (with piccolo extra to two flutes, three trombones plus tuba, three drums and harp) seems to have held on leash, not slipped, the coursing thoughts of the composer. There is some attractive scoring : a typical wood-wind nasal noise at the opening; oboe lead against low strings (Ex. 6); trumpets, first fiddles, and piccolo in three octaves to intensify the mood (Ex. 7); and finally an interesting part for the drum which plays in the rhythm ♩ 𝄽 𝄽 ♩ 𝄽 for twenty-three bars, marked first piano, then sempre più piano and later diminuendo, *pp* and *ppp*—all this in the first of the Dances. In the second Dance, the lovely haunting tune with its typical folk-style repeats is given to us by the oboe above low strings (violas and 'cellos *divisi* and the basses pizzicato) with harp (Ex. 8). Octave higher strings, with bass still pizzicato, against held wind chords, are used for the second statement. Later we find wood-wind trills—uncommon in Grieg : and there are charming effects at letter E with piccolo, flute and oboe (Ex. 9).

All through this piece, the scoring still leans towards the separating of colours. The third Dance[1] shows this even more : e.g. the minor transformation of the second melodic idea[2] is given on wind above

[1] It is worth observing that the opening declamatory phrase of this third Dance is, note for note, the same as the ejaculation of the soloist at the beginning of the Piano Concerto. An obvious *improvisatore* violin passage, it is interesting as showing Grieg's great interest in the folk-player of the violin, throughout his life, for this motive is one of his commonest fingerprints.

[2] Similarly Ex. 6 in the first Dance is a rhythmic transformation, in the minor, of the opening major theme.

pizzicato bass first of all, and then on first and second violins, violas and 'cellos in octaves, against a counterpoint on wood-wind and horns and quiet drums. The fourth Dance is the most developed, based mainly on a magnificent marching folk-tune. The composer appears to overreach himself here. The large-scale use of the orchestra seems to fog him slightly : though it is very loud and grand and noble (and there is some nice string scoring), the total effect is not entirely successful. The più tranquillo middle section is charming.

Den Bergtekne is the only song that Grieg conceived originally with orchestral accompaniment, though he orchestrated some of his other song-accompaniments, including *En Svane* and *Fra Monte Pincio*; it is laid out for strings with two horns, and should be very effective; Miss Desmond deals with it more fully in a later chapter.[1] The *Two Lyric Pieces*, from Op. 68, demand a solo horn and a solo oboe for the first number only, *Evening in the Mountains*. This is a curious and remote pastoral piece. The two wind instruments play a picture at the opening, the oboe singing to us a mountain (unaccompanied) chant (Ex. 10) that makes Wagner look more than usually sophisticated and Berlioz's *Scène aux champs* like a picture by Claude. They have only recapitulary phrases at the end.

The remaining works for orchestra are for strings alone : the beautiful *Two Elegiac Melodies*, the *Two Melodies* on songs of his own, the *Holberg* Suite, and the *Two Norwegian Tunes*. The two first-named works sound very lovely, and are exquisite in craftsmanship. The *Two Elegiac Melodies*, for string orchestra, are, for some reason best known to conductors, the pieces they choose for their programmes. Good as they are, they give no excuse for neglect of the other string works. These two pieces are based on song-settings of poems by Vinje, Op. 33, Nos. 2 and 3. Both are charmingly scored for strings, but there is so little change in the musical content that it is not worth while quoting Grieg's string versions. But it may be mentioned that in the second piece, he scores on a very wide range, covering a big harmonic field of sound with his seemingly sparse forces. The *Holberg* Suite is more vigorous and forthright : in fact, it might be held to be Grieg's second most important orchestral work after the Piano Concerto. Not planned on the scale of the *Symphonic Dances*, it yet bids fair to rival them in achieving the really big scale. Ludwig Holberg, ' the Molière of the North ', died in 1684, and two hundred years later Grieg (among other Scandinavian composers) wrote music in his commemoration. He seems to have been inspired

[1] See page 86.

by the task, and he wrote—originally for piano—this splendid 'old-time' suite. Only, of course, it was not 'old-time'; it was the real Grieg. The five movements are not equal : none is easy to play, asking for an orchestra of experience, and if possible of some dimensions. From the point of view of the present chapter, the main interest lies in Grieg's ingenious scoring of the peculiarly pianistic passages of the Prelude (cf. Ex. 11a and b).

High in colour-values as Grieg's orchestral music is, there is far less local colour than one would expect from a composer so nationalist in his idiom. True, a preference is shown for the oboe above the clarinet : elsewhere than in the unaccompanied recitative of the first of the *Two Lyric Pieces*, Op. 68, the pastoral quality of the oboe tone is exploited. A typical passage (they abound) is the oboe lead in the *Symphonic Dance* No. 1 quoted as Ex. 6 and another in No. 3 (Ex. 12) which also shows Grieg's fondness for the stringed fifth (open strings for preference). This fondness extends to the sister instrument, the bassoon : an instrument for which Grieg wrote interesting parts (for example, in the Piano Concerto, *passim*, and of course *Morning* in *Peer Gynt*). The piccolo is scored for in the *Symphonic Dances*, *Autumn* overture, *Bergljot*, and the *Peer Gynt* and *Sigurd Jorsalfar* suites (see *Symphonic Dance* No. 2, where the piccolo has a charming part quoted in Ex. 9); but nowhere is there a call for a cor anglais or a bass clarinet. Trills or shakes on the wood-wind occur sparsely, the most notable case is again in the second *Symphonic Dance* towards the end.

Of the brass instruments, Grieg favoured the horns and trombones above the trumpets. He never writes for three trumpets, but always for three trombones plus tuba. Yet there is little sonorous writing for brass : here is the opposite of Wagnerian practice. Even in long crescendos, the intensification is made as much by repeated notes on the strings and octave doublings as by piling up the brass. The fortissimos, excellently planned as they are, lack resonance.

As for percussion, apart from the early overture, it is used singularly little. There is the famous triangle in *Anitra's Dance* (Ex. 13) against muted strings, and the drum passage referred to above in the first *Symphonic Dance*; also an interesting passage in No. 4 where strings and drums alternate with short notes thus :

'Celli and Timp :
Double Bass :

But on the whole Grieg's use of percussion can be called elementary.

23

There is, too, a noticeable rarity of plucked sounds: there is a harp part in the *Symphonic Dances*, effectively written: but there is singularly little writing for pizzicato strings.

The orchestral medium which Grieg found most sympathetic and expressive for his ideas was, of course, the string family. A detailed study of his string writing is very illuminating: elaborate though it is, it is never fussy and always precise. Thus he asks for nine solo players only in *Anitra's Dance*, and in the *Arabian Dance* in *Peer Gynt* he gives in a note a direction that the pizzicato chords must not be played arpeggio. Three points stand out at once: a love of doubling strings at the octave (sometimes with three octaves), a frequent use of contrast between upper and lower registers, and a habit of writing short, lightly bowed notes with a rest afterwards, a crotchet being often notated ♪ ⸗ or even 𝅘𝅥 ⸗ .. This last helps to keep Grieg's texture light and clear. At the same time, it will be observed that there are far fewer expression marks than are commonly found in the nineteenth century.

A few passages may be named as showing some methods of getting string effects typical of Grieg's scoring. The frequent doubling of melody at the octave is early apparent in the Piano Concerto (first and second movements), where, too, the rests are an important feature of the score; also in *Two Norwegian Melodies*, with elaborate divisi effects on 'cellos (Ex. 14); and again in the *Symphonic Dances*, especially in Nos. 2 and 3. For examples of deliberate alternation of registers I may quote from the second of the *Two Lyric Pieces* (from Op. 68), where the melody of *By the Cradle* is first stated in four-part harmony by the first and second violins divisi, the first violin taking the lowest voice (Ex. 15); later, the lower strings join in. The mysterious low strings at letter B of the Piano Concerto, third movement (p. 72 of the Eulenburg score), the four divisi 'cellos at the opening of the *Homage March* from *Sigurd Jorsalfar* (Ex. 16) and the dark colouring of *Ingrid's Lament* (*Peer Gynt*) (Ex. 17) are other cases.

Grieg was fond, too, of using a solo 'cello for special effects: see Piano Concerto, third movement, second subject, and *Holberg* Suite throughout, especially Nos. 2, 4 and 5.

I have not cited more passages from the *Holberg* Suite simply because the work abounds in magnificent string effects; also, it is more frequently played than the other pieces. The Sarabande (No. 2) is particularly worth careful study, with its opening in four-part harmony for second violins and violas only, the 'cello and low first violins only coming in at the fifth bar (Ex. 18); later there is a fine effect with solo 'cello and first violins in unison, second violins on the alto line, and violas doubling the melody at the lower octave; observe also the characteristic divisi 'cellos in the continuation (Ex. 19). The whole work is a continuing source of beautiful sounds, but it should be repeated that it is not a work suitable for small amateur orchestras, though it is frequently played by them. The work is, on the contrary, Grieg's most carefully elaborated piece of orchestration, despite the fact that it is confined to strings.

In very brief conclusion, it may be added that the field of pure orchestral music was not one that Grieg tilled easily, or even willingly, yet he produced from it a rich if small harvest. His precise mind fitted the orchestral clothing with absolute exactness to the ideas expressed. His orchestration is in scale the equivalent of his musical thought : and as such, it is high art.

3

The Piano Concerto

By

Gerald Abraham

M<small>R. FOSS HAS DISCUSSED</small> points in the orchestration of the Piano Concerto; it will be touched on again in the chapter on Grieg's piano music and elsewhere; but the Concerto is neither an orchestral work nor a piano composition and, familiar though it is, it demands at least brief consideration as what it is: a piece for piano and orchestra, and Grieg's most ambitious instrumental composition at that. I think it marks a crisis, an end, in Grieg's development as a composer. It is Op. 16. Consider the previous opus numbers, which are in Grieg's case generally much less misleading than usual on points of chronological order. True there are a number of songs and small piano pieces, but look at the others:

Op. 7. Piano Sonata.
Op. 8. F major Violin Sonata.
Op. 11. *Autumn* Overture.
Op. 13. G major Violin Sonata.
Op. 14. The remains of a Symphony in C minor.

Those are the ' first period ' works of a young man who is setting out on a career as a large-scale composer. Then at twenty-five came the A minor Concerto, and after it—during all the remaining forty years of Grieg's life—he managed to finish only three more full-scale sonata-sized instrumental works. There is another significant change after the Concerto. Up to then the genuine or closely imitated folk-element in Grieg's music had been very slight, limited to a couple of *Lyric Pieces* and one or two of the themes of the second Violin Sonata; there is a Norwegian quality in some of this earlier music, but it probably derives second-hand from Ole Bull and Nordraak as much as first-hand from the people. But in 1869, the year after the A minor Concerto, Grieg discovered Lindeman's great collection of folk-tunes *Aeldre og nyere fjeldmelodier*, from which he at once arranged twenty-five songs and dances for piano as his Op. 17 and which until the eighteen-nineties remained his chief, if not his only, source for Norwegian popular melody. But once having found it, he drew on it very heavily; the G minor Ballade for piano, the *Old Norwegian Melody with variations* for two pianos, the *Norwegian Dances* for piano duet (bar one theme), the *Symphonic Dances*—that is to say, practically all his most characteristic larger instrumental works of the later period—are entirely based on themes from Lindeman's collection.

The A minor Concerto, then, is a real milestone in Grieg's career, the last and best work of his early ' sonata ' period. It seems to have decided him, effectively if not finally, that his forte was for the miniature, not the large-scale work. And that is the final æsthetic judgment on the Concerto—whether we deplore Grieg's failure to overcome his weakness as a large-scale musical architect or applaud the wisdom that decided him to keep to that which he could do well—that it is essentially a mosaic of unrelated lyrical miniatures or materials for lyrical pieces, charming in themselves though sometimes unhappily inflated in scoring and dynamics to produce something like the climaxes that a large-scale work must have (cf. pp. 59–60 and 112–3 of the Eulenburg miniature score).

Yet, historically considered, Grieg's work is an excellent specimen of its genre : the nineteenth-century heroic-romantic piano concerto, which differs fundamentally from the classical concerto with its double exposition in the first movement. Grieg, like most other later nineteenth-century composers, cheerfully ignored all the subtle possibilities of the classical concerto and simply wrote a first movement in sonata-form for piano and orchestra. I am obliged to add that he equally cheerfully ignored all the subtle possibilities of sonata-form, making his recapitulation almost a literal repetition of his exposition—except for the necessary change of modulation to the second subject —and not even bothering to change the relationship of soloist and orchestra. In the revised version of the score which he made just before his death, he even wiped out little differences of instrumentation that had existed in the original version. Sonata-form was to Grieg simply a convenient, though inconveniently large, frame over which to spread a number of ideas; it was never the skeleton of a living organism.

Even the details of the frame were to some extent copied from the first movement of the Schumann Concerto in the same key. In both movements we find an introductory chordal passage for the soloist, descending from the high to the middle register. In both, the main theme is then stated by the wind and repeated exactly by the soloist; both naturally have the second subject in the relative major, though Grieg does not follow Schumann in fashioning first and second subjects from the same basic idea (as he was to do later in the G minor Quartet); both expositions conclude with an animato; both developments fall into two main sections in the first of which wood-wind soli play with fragments of the main theme over piano arpeggios, while the soloist comes to the fore in the second (in Schumann the two sections are separated by a short dialogue on the introductory passage); in both the cadenza is followed by a coda quicker than the rest of the movement, Schumann's on a new form of the motto-theme, Grieg's on an entirely new theme. There is no resemblance between the actual ideas; it was simply that Grieg, at the highest stage of his development as a composer in sonata-form, still felt the need for a formal model.

Once in later life, in 1883, Grieg was tempted to begin a second Piano Concerto, in B minor. He made sketches for the first and third movements but, as he told his publisher, 'Pegasus wouldn't budge.' and he let them lie; excerpts from them were published posthumously by his friend Julius Röntgen in his report on 'Grieg's musical remains' in *Die Musik*.[1] The first movement begins with an orchestral introduction; the soloist enters with a cadenza-like passage and then states the first subject proper, which I quote as Ex. 20. The opening of the finale is given as Ex. 21.

Instead of writing a companion to the A minor Concerto, Grieg could only tinker with his completed masterpiece. He was dissatisfied with the original scoring, which is sometimes rather crude, and he had against his better judgment accepted Liszt's advice on a number of details before publication, notably the giving of the second subject of the first movement in both exposition and recapitulation to a solo trumpet instead of to the 'cellos. We hear more than once in his letters of revisions to the score and during the very last year of his life he completed a final revision which left the Concerto in the form we always hear to-day. The changes in the solo part are few and unimportant but those in the scoring are numerous and sometimes drastic, and comparison is very interesting. I list only the more important differences, with page and bar references to the easily accessible Eulenburg miniature score of the final version:

> p. 3. As Mr. Foss has already remarked, the original score has only two horns but includes a tuba. Bar 1 begins with a pizzicato

[1] Jahrgang VII, No. 5.

tonic chord which, as it were, releases the drum roll; this is supported by horns and tuba. There is no tutti chord in bar 2; the piano enters alone.

p. 4. Slight differences in the lay-out of the piano arpeggio and chords; the quaver octaves in bar 2 are E, not G sharp.

p. 7. In bars 5–6 the D and G of the second violins are repeated crotchets; the 'cellos are not divided and play only the lower notes.

pp. 12–13. The oboe echo of the piano, after letter B, was originally played by the first flute, doubled by the first clarinet an octave lower; instead of the dotted minim in the third bar after B, the melodic movement is continued.

p. 14. The appearance of the second subject on the trumpet, with the other changes of scoring, are shown as Ex. 22; note the marking ' Tempo lento ' instead of ' Più lento '.

p. 15. In bars 2 and 4 the strings all rest after the first beat; upper string parts are altered in bar 3.

p. 19. The ' Animato ' marking is absent.

pp. 20–21. The string tremolos are double-stops; minor changes in horn and viola parts.

p. 22. Different lay-out of string and trombone parts.

p. 23. *Molto* tranquillo. In bars 1–2 the present flute part is played by first clarinet with flute an octave higher; instead of the horn echoing them in bars 3–4, they echo themselves an octave lower. Originally the horn strengthened the viola part on this page, the violas themselves playing triplet quavers like the violins. 'Cellos pizzicato; double-basses tacent.

p. 24. Trombones instead of horns; bassoons double 'cellos instead of double-basses (again in parallel passage on next page). In bars 5–6, clarinet (with flute octave higher) instead of horn.

p. 25. No ' a tempo ' marking. Wood-wind instead of horns and trumpet; different lay-out of trombone parts.

p. 27. Bar 1: flute instead of oboe. In bar 2 (and bar 1 of p. 28) violas double the trombones and remaining strings play the triplet E.

p. 29. *et seq.* Most of the scoring in the recapitulation is the same as in the exposition. The only interesting difference is pp. 34–35; here the oboe plays as in the definitive version, except that it has one more triplet with grace-notes to fill out bar 1 of p. 35, but it is doubled by first bassoon an octave lower. The pedal E is strengthened by horns and drum-roll.

p. 46. The cadenza ends differently. Last bar of page: simple trill on G sharp for one beat; rest of the bar and whole of the next bar simple octave trills on B, and then into the tutti.

p. 47. The strings are not divided; they play only the upper parts; but first violins are doubled an octave lower by clarinets, 'cellos by bassoons.

p. 52. Bars 2–5, first horn doubles the 'cellos; bars 6–8, first bassoon doubles the violas—there is no ' cresc. ed accel.' marking. The striking horn entry in bar 9, one of the most memorable points in the whole score, is lacking; so, too, is the continuation of the horn melody by a solo 'cello; the present horn and solo 'cello line is played by first violins.

p. 55. No tranquillo marking; slightly different lay-out of lower strings.

p. 57. No tranquillo marking. Various minor changes in string parts; holding note added for horn. In the passage beginning with the last bar of the page, the oboe part is played by flute, the bassoon by clarinet.

pp. 58–61. The two bars before letter B have slightly different wind scoring. The passage beginning at letter B is quite differently scored: even the piano part and the harmony are changed on the third beat of the last bar on p. 59. Flute and clarinet in octaves double the piano melody; the phrase on first 'cellos and first bassoon is missing—or, rather, only vaguely adumbrated in the first violin part. The little clarinet interjection on p. 61 is missing.

p. 62. Minor changes in string parts.

p. 63. Bars 3–4: both flutes play first flute part an octave lower; oboe tacet; clarinets play only the lower part; first bassoon part played by solo horn and 'cellos. In bars 5–6 there is a string accompaniment, first violins doubling the piano melody an octave lower. Last bar: the lento crotchets for piano are lacking.

p. 64. Bars 1–4, no pizzicato chords; wood-wind all play an octave lower.

p. 65. Different lay-out of tutti chord.

p. 66. Horn supported by drum in A.

p. 67. Minor changes in violin and bassoon parts.

p. 70. Last bar, phrase for oboe and bassoon missing (though, as they have it in the parallel passage on p. 94, this may be an error).

p. 71. Bar 4 *et seq.*: first violins play in crotchets *on* the beat.

pp. 73–75. First oboe instead of first clarinet; bassoons and horn tacent; whole-bar rests for violins filled in; double-basses pizzicato.

pp. 76–78. Brass parts rewritten.

p. 79. *et seq.* Cellos reinforced by horns on their repeated notes in the second half of the bar.

p. 81. No animato at letter D; changes in wood-wind and bass trombone parts.

p. 82. Bars 2–4, flutes double first oboe. Bars 5 *et seq.* no poco rit. or poco più tranquillo marking. No held chord for wood-wind in bars 5–8; the chord is given instead to strings tremolo in the same register, and they accompany the flute solo in the low register instead of an octave higher, sul ponticello, as in the final score. The first clarinet doubles the flute an octave lower. The same scoring persists on p. 83.

p. 87. Bars 1–3 Un poco, instead of molto, ritard. No 'a tempo' marking at bar 5, or perdendosi rit. at bar 11.

p. 88.   Alterations as in parallel passages earlier, except that in the passage beginning with the penultimate bar on p. 94 it is the first bassoon which doubles the piano melody an octave lower.

p. 99.   Sostenuto, instead of meno allegro; con fuoco, instead of con forza. The bassoons double the violins (except for the upward rushes of hemidemisemiquavers); only first flute and first clarinet play, instead of à 2.

p. 100.   Bar 4 *et seq.* the clarinets double the violin parts instead of playing holding notes; the bassoon-horn chord is laid out differently.

p. 102.   Different lay-out of bassoon and horn parts.

pp. 106–107.   Horns tacent; double basses tacent during the last four bars of p. 106.

pp. 110–111.   Flutes and oboes tacent; clarinet, bassoon and horn chords differently laid out. Bar 2 *et seq.* of p. 111: first trumpet octave higher; trills on all strings; sostenuto, instead of poco rit.

pp. 112–115.   Maestoso, instead of andante maestoso. No piccolo; bass trombone reinforced by tuba. The melody is played by trumpets (unison) and first and second trombones (octaves) only; wood-wind and 'cellos take part in the harmonic background. Strings and horns, both marked *ff* like the wood-wind, show various differences: first violins are not divided, second violins have B instead of D on first half of bar 2, violas are a sixth to an octave lower, etc.

p. 115.   Bars 1–2, the piano part has been re-written.

p. 116.   No poco rit. or 'a tempo' markings. The melody on p. 116 is played by violins, horns and trumpets; first and second trombones join the harmonic background; wood-wind and viola parts changed.

It would certainly not be worth anyone's trouble to resurrect the original version in the concert hall. Most of the changes are unquestionably improvements. But if we want to know what sort of orchestrator Grieg was as a young man, we must look at the original edition, not at the miniature score.

4

The Chamber Music

By

Alan Frank

THE SURPRISING THING ABOUT Grieg's chamber-music output is not that it was small but that it comprised as many works as it did, and that these works were spread fairly evenly over a large proportion of his composing career. Grieg completed five chamber works: three Violin Sonatas, a 'Cello Sonata, and a String Quartet. He thus wrote more works in this medium than did several other composers who more readily come to mind when one considers non-German chamber music of the latter half of the nineteenth century, more for example than Smetana (two Quartets and a Piano Trio), Borodin (two Quartets), or Franck (a Violin Sonata, a Quartet, and a Piano Quintet, excluding some very early works). These works by Grieg cannot be ascribed to a short 'chamber music period' in his life —as in the instance of Schumann, the bulk if not all of whose finest chamber works were composed in one year.[1] Grieg's early first Violin Sonata was written in 1865, the second two years later, and the third, his last completed chamber work, in 1887.[2] Between the second and third Violin Sonatas come the String Quartet of 1877–8 and the 'Cello Sonata of 1883. So while it cannot be denied that Grieg was not naturally a composer in the chamber-music medium, his output cannot be written off as occasional capricious experimenting on his part. Moreover, it should be remembered that aside from his chamber music Grieg wrote only three full-length works of sonata or symphonic type: the early Piano Sonata, the unpublished Symphony and the Piano Concerto.

It is clear then that Grieg, absorbed though he was by the two mediums for which his special gifts suited him, namely songs and

[1] A more curious case is that of Grieg's compatriot, Svendsen, to whom he dedicated his second Violin Sonata. Svendsen wrote three chamber works in his twenties and then nothing else in this medium for the remaining forty-three years of his life. W. W. Cobbett darkly remarks that ' his mode of life was not favourable to serious work '.

[2] Two movements of an incomplete String Quartet are later still, being dated 1891.

32

short piano pieces, was not unattracted by the possibilities of writing chamber music. At least two of his chamber works, the third Violin Sonata and the 'Cello Sonata (they are in fact the best) were at one time immensely popular and widely played, overplayed maybe. They have now dropped out of the concert repertoire, and Grieg's contribution to chamber music is almost forgotten. Justly or unjustly? It cannot be held that Grieg as a composer is just out of fashion temporarily, since then the Piano Concerto would have suffered the same eclipse. Nor can it be argued that we are to-day so bound to the strict nineteenth-century German concepts of sonata-form and construction that we refuse to accept works which depart from those concepts. Schubert, like Grieg an essentially lyrical composer, would by such standards be regarded as unorthodox ' if it were not that composers of Schubert's stature shape their own orthodoxy '.[1] Similarly we do not criticise Grieg because in place of a normal slow movement he substitutes a simple, short ' romance '. On the contrary Grieg could with impunity have allowed himself considerably more freedom in handling the design of his chamber music. And here, I think, lies the explanation of its weakness and lack of staying power so far as public performance is concerned.

Frequently in examining and hearing Grieg's chamber works, one is astounded that a composer of such imagination and freshness—and even in the weakest movements these qualities are not absent—should have allowed himself to lapse into prolonged passages of uninventive, facile hack music. There is no other description. This stricture applies exclusively to his first and last movements. These are extended fast movements, and if it is admitted that, firstly, Grieg was more drawn to a particular type of slowish tranquillo tune than to an allegro theme, and, secondly, he was by temperament incapable of, or uninterested in, ' extending ' (that is, developing) his musical ideas, then it becomes quite understandable that such movements are not wholly successful. This judgment, which summarises rather baldly the commonest criticism of his chamber music, is largely correct. But it begs the question why Grieg, who surely was as aware of his limitations as he was of his gifts, the one complementing the other, elected to cast two movements of each of his chamber works in rather conventional length and shape. Furthermore, one cannot pass judgment so easily on Grieg without being faced by the problem of the Piano Concerto.

[1] J. A. Westrup in the ' Chamber Music ' chapter of *Schubert: a symposium* (Lindsay Drummond, 1947).

It is illuminating to turn to the first movement of this work, in which the faults of parallel movements in the chamber music are almost entirely absent. Here Grieg did write a full-length movement with little or no sign of padding. There is freedom and imagination in development, of a fantasia type, inspired partly by the facilities offered by orchestral colour but far more by the fact that Grieg was using the piano as a solo instrument. Notice for example the freshness and growth of the piano passages immediately following the orchestral expositions of the first and second subjects; and how, when the recapitulation is just in danger of becoming overlong by repetition, the piano cadenza intervenes to save the movement and give added impetus to the coda. Or again, in the last movement, how the piano is allowed to flow freely on when it first takes over the second subject after its statement by the orchestra.

Seldom in the longer movements of the sonatas does one come across any similar freedom in the use of the piano, or the effects of spontaneity which arise in the Piano Concerto through easy interplay of piano and orchestral instruments. The problems are of course different. The sonatas are duets for two instruments of equal status. Grieg could not, and did not, overshadow the stringed instrument by over-indulging the piano. But neither did he attain a convincing musical fusion between the two instruments. His most frequent device in this direction was to employ imitational writing, which at times becomes mechanical and tiresome. He had none of the genius of a Franck for sustained canonical writing. Too often, in addition, the musical interest in the sonatas lies in one instrument or the other, but not in both. Such procedure is justified at times in such simple works as these, but simplicity is not to be confused with dullness (and there are many passages of accompaniment which it must be confessed are dull). The almost total absence of real interweaving between the instruments gives a choppy effect to the movements as a whole, and prevents them from achieving the stature which their length demands. Similar lack of interplay between first and second subjects in the development also contributes to this effect.

The other problem, of imparting unity to a work in several movements, Grieg with one exception did not attempt to solve by structural device. The exception is the String Quartet where a motto-theme is recurrent in all four movements, and a quotation from the third movement occurs in the finale. The effect is forced and its somewhat heavy formalism is out of style with the musical content of the work. The unity is superimposed rather than integrated. Of the other works the third Violin Sonata makes the most satisfactory whole. The previous Violin Sonata has a last movement which so closely resembles the first movement in theme, rhythm, and harmony (see Exs. 35 and 36) that it proves inadequate as a sonata finale; while the 'Cello Sonata and the first Violin Sonata have last movements which are noticeably the weakest in the works. Possibly conscious of this, Grieg attempts to strengthen the latter by a fugato episode (see Ex. 38) rare in his music and reminding one that he did study at Leipzig. In itself the episode is not ineffective but in its context it appears somewhat anomalous.

Thus, in general, the chamber works are enjoyable more for their parts than as complete three- or four-movement creations. They all contain much that is typical and representative of Grieg: in their harmonies, their tunefulness, and their lively, unsophisticated rhythms. Their best qualities emerge when Grieg ceases to be oppressed by the formalistic and other difficulties of writing a full-length work, and is able to be most characteristically himself: for instance, in the slow movements and the lyrical second subjects of the fast movements. The charm and freshness here are such as to make one regret that Grieg did not write any small-scale compositions, *Lyric Pieces*, *Holberg* Suites and the like, for chamber-music combinations instead of attempting full-length works. What a delight to professional or amateur wind players, for example, would have been a series of simple Grieg pieces for perhaps clarinet, or oboe, or horn and piano. (Schumann, whose music Grieg greatly admired, did write several such pieces.) Admittedly this is idle speculation, but it does raise a point pertinent to any consideration of Grieg's music: its suitability for amateur performers. In the case of the chamber music, whatever its merits or weaknesses on the concert platform, it remains ideal material for playing in the home. There is little enough in late nineteenth-century music which can be tackled by players of modest technical attainments. There are certainly few sonatas for a stringed instrument and piano which sound as attractive as Grieg's do in the hands of amateur players.

Grieg was not a string player, unlike so many nineteenth-century composers[1]; but he wrote well for strings, as is evident not only in the chamber music but in the brilliantly scored *Holberg* Suite. In his earlier years Grieg had come much under the influence of the Norwegian violinist, Ole Bull, and played chamber music with him

---

[1] For instance Schubert, Mendelssohn, Dvořák, Borodin, and among Scandinavian composers, Svendsen, Sinding, Gade.

and with his own brother, John Grieg, an amateur 'cellist to whom the 'Cello Sonata is dedicated. The string writing in this work and in the Violin Sonatas, especially No. 3, is consistently effective. The only work in which the string writing is technically open to criticism is the String Quartet in G minor. Here a straining after orchestral effect is shown in the use of all four instruments playing simultaneously for bars on end in double or triple-stopping. In the much later unfinished Quartet the writing is noticeably freer from such thickness, which is unsuited to chamber-music style, and for that matter to Grieg's personal idiom.

In the following examination of the chamber works in greater detail, I have not attempted an equally full analysis of each of them. To subject them all to such a process would be inappropriate and unprofitable. On the other hand it is even more unprofitable to brush aside any suggestion of criticism in a welter of Grieg-adulation, since by glossing over the works' weaknesses their positive attractions also pass unnoticed. The lengthy study of Grieg in English by Henry T. Finck is notorious in this respect. Biographically it contains material of considerable interest; musically it is of little value. Of Grieg as a chamber-music composer, the author writes: '. . . qualitatively he belongs in the first rank. In the concert halls of the future it is safe to predict that no music of this class will be played more frequently than his superb string quartet and his no less admirable sonatas for piano and violin.' Events have so firmly belied this prophecy that particularly to younger players and students to-day some of these works are virtually unknown. This brief discussion of them may therefore serve a double purpose: of recalling the works to those who have known and have partially forgotten them, and of presenting them to those who, *pace* Mr. Finck, are aware of the works through hearsay only.

Of the three Violin Sonatas, the last (Op. 45 in C minor) is, as I have pointed out above, the finest; it is indeed the most satisfactory of all the chamber works. It exhibits a strength and dramatic sweep, especially in its first movement, to which the earlier Violin Sonatas do not aspire. The intensity of the opening theme (Ex. 23) is pointed by its being announced without any prefatory bar or bars; it is almost unique in this respect among Grieg's sonata openings. A subsidiary melodic figure of a calmer character, not used in later development, enters on the violin at bar 23 but soon gives way to the return of the main theme, now accompanied chordally in the rhythm: ♩♪♩♪|♩♪♩♪ etc. This rhythm anticipates the accompaniment of

the second subject, in E flat (Ex. 24). The structure of this theme
reveals a characteristic common to many of Grieg's slower tunes, so
common that, were Grieg a less essentially intuitive composer, one
would describe it as a mechanical process. The third and fourth bars
are an elaborated repeat of the first and second bars, while bars 5–8
are again an elaboration of bars 3–4. Thus an eight-bar phrase grows
from the first two bars, in this instance from the two notes G and
B flat. The second subject is treated at some length in the exposition
but does not figure in the development section. This section opens
promisingly, with a version of the main theme, now in major key,
augmented, and revealed in quite fresh light by its setting. Ex.
25 shows this transformation which is one of the most agreeable
passages in the work. In bars 6–7 occurs the Grieg melodic 'hall-
mark' already mentioned by Mr. Foss, the three descending notes:
tonic, seventh, dominant (in this case, B flat, A, F). For readers
interested in identifying this 'hall-mark' in the chamber music (it
is common throughout all his music), other instances quoted will
be seen in Exs. 26, 31, 34, 40, 41, 44, 46, 48, 49, 50, 51. The music
continues in the lay-out of Ex. 25 through a variety of keys—
B flat major, B flat minor, A major, A minor, etc.—with the descending semitonal bass maintained. A falling semitone also plays a
notable part in subsequent, and not especially inspired, development,
and again in the accompaniment to a molto animato working of the
first two bars of the main subject. After a climactic reference to this
subject in augmentation, similar to Ex. 25 but in sixths double-
stopped, the recapitulation begins. As is usual with Grieg, this
follows the exposition exactly, with the second subject now in the
tonic, instead of relative, major. Previous material based on this
subject is repeated but shortened, Ex. 25 reappears in A flat, also
shortened, and a bridge passage leads into a final presto, formed from
the main subject.

The second movement is a simple Allegretto espressivo alla
Romanza, showing Grieg at his happiest. It is in E major, and is
the only example among the chamber works of a movement in a
key not closely related to that of the first movement. (The identical
sequence of keys occurs in the Piano Concerto: first movement A
minor, slow movement D flat major.) There is no attempt to 'mix'
the two instruments, and the movement starts with 44 bars of piano
only (see Ex. 34 for the opening), followed by the same number of
bars where the violin repeats exactly the melodic line of the previous
piano section over simple chordal accompaniment. After these 88

bars in E major, a contrasted quick 2/4 section, in E minor, of Norwegian dance type, appears. As this fades out a scale passage on the dominant of E major prepares one for the return of the alla Romanza in its original key. But instead, the original tune returns in E flat, the recurrence of the E major key being suspended for another eight bars. I quote the whole passage (Ex. 26) as showing that Grieg's harmonic schemes, simple though they are, cannot always be taken for granted. The appassionato chordal triplets of the piano continue to accompany the violin's re-statement of the opening tune, and a coda is characterised by ascending violin trills above the piano's descending chromatic bass. Such contrary motion between highest and lowest parts occurs frequently in Grieg (another example appears in the prestissimo which closes this work).

The last movement, like that of the second Violin Sonata, is built in two sections, as follows:

First section: first subject in C minor, stated on the violin and repeated by the piano in C minor; second subject (which throughout the movement is heard only on the violin) in A flat.

Second section: first subject in C minor, repeated in F minor; second subject in C major, coda in C major.

The first subject (Ex. 27) lends itself to a good deal of rather naïve imitation between the two instruments. After the piano has repeated it, with the imitational figure transferred to the violin, the C–G–C' quavers of the accompaniment are changed suddenly to C–G flat–C', and a powerful crescendo leads to a major version, marcato (Ex. 28), of the main theme. After an unexpected brief incursion into E minor, the harmonically arresting second subject appears (Ex. 29). This pattern continues for another 72 bars, the melodic interest remaining in the violin and no attempt being made to vary the predominant rhythm, ♪♩♩ , of the piano. One is more than ready for the return to C minor, Tempo I, indicating the beginning of the second section. This follows Ex. 27 but with the piano fifths in the left hand omitted, and continues as repetition of the first section apart from the variation of key already mentioned. When the second subject appears, Grieg makes amends for his earlier lack of enterprise in its treatment, and it is heard in a much transformed setting, the theme itself being slightly modified in rhythm. I quote the first few bars which are sufficient to show the scheme (Ex. 30). It continues for rather shorter length than that of the corresponding part of the first section, and leads to a prestissimo coda based on the opening bars of the main theme.

The two previous Violin Sonatas are much more uneven, though particularly the second (Op. 13 in G), which Liszt admired, has good things in it. Alone among the sonatas it opens with a slow introduction, in G minor, the violin rhapsodically foreshadowing the first subject. In this introduction occurs one of the freshest ideas of the whole work but no use is subsequently made of it. It lasts for eight bars, of which Ex. 31 shows the first four, bars 3 and 4 being once again a typical elaboration of bars 1 and 2. At the allegro the main G major subject is announced by piano alone (Ex. 35 shows the theme) and not taken up by the violin until after a temporary transition into E flat. In all other fast movements of the sonatas the violin is given the initial statement of the main theme. The tranquillo second subject in B minor, though not one of Grieg's most striking tunes, is treated at length, being repeated—after a laborious pedal passage rhythmically based on bar 3 of the main theme—in D major, *ff* sostenuto. The development section is on the weak side and, short though it is, lapses into padding, of which Ex. 32 gives one instance. The recapitulation omits the previous opening of the allegro and takes up from the violin's statement of the first subject. Otherwise only minor changes of previous material are made.

The song-like slow movement is of greater appeal and is comparable to that of the third Violin Sonata in shape and key (E minor with contrasted middle section in E major and return of E minor section: in the third Violin Sonata the sequence is in E major, E minor, E major). Also there is strong thematic resemblance; Ex. 33 shows the opening of the major section of this Sonata, Ex. 34 the opening of the slow movement of the third Sonata.

The finale's main theme unfortunately resembles that of the first movement very closely in rhythm and harmony. To the enthusiast for Norwegian folk-dance it may be ' a genuine *springer*, full of youthful enthusiasm, vigour, and joy of life '[1] but that does not make it an adequate conclusion to a sonata. Ex. 36 quotes the opening of the theme and its accompaniment, Ex. 35 gives the theme of the first movement which as the reader can verify fits as well over the accompaniment of Ex. 36. Perhaps this is cheating but, whatever the reason, much of this finale has a monotonous effect, though relieved by two pleasant subsidiary themes, stated in the first section in respectively B minor and E flat (tranquillo and *pp*). The second section of the movement, as in the parallel movement of the third

---

[1] *Cobbett's Cyclopedic Survey of Chamber Music* (Oxford University Press)

Sonata, repeats the first section until the tranquillo theme, now played *ff* sostenuto in G. A 14-bar presto—no more than a chordal flourish—provides a tame end to the work.

Of the youthful first Violin Sonata (Op. 8 in F) the middle movement, a type of minuet (there is no slow movement proper), is the only one of interest as being characteristic of Grieg. The other two movements are distinctly academic, as is the Piano Sonata of the same period, with formal repeats of the exposition sections and empty development passages. From the last movement I quote an all-too-typical piece of uninspired imitational writing (Ex. 37), and, more as a curiosity than for any other reason, the 15-bar fugato (Ex. 38) which appears immediately after the double-bar and to which I have referred above (p. 35).

Except for a falling-off in the last movement, the 'Cello Sonata in A minor, Op. 36, approaches the standard of the third Violin Sonata. It is extremely well written for 'cello, with variety of texture in the piano part. In the opening movement both first and second subjects (Ex. 39 and bar 9 *et seq.* of Ex. 40) are good 'cello tunes, the former being dramatically treated in the course of the movement. Both subjects are formed according to the Grieg 'elaboration' pattern already mentioned (compare bars 4 and 1 of Ex. 39; bars 11–12 and 9–10 of Ex. 40). In the longish exposition and in development much use is made of the repeated minims of the first subject, the opening notes being altered from EFE to three emphatic repeated E's. If some of the character of the theme is thereby lost, it none the less provides the basis of the pleasant bridge passage leading to the second subject, as Ex. 40 shows. Less inspired are the imitational use to which this variant of the first subject is put, and later its employment above a dominant pedal lasting for 28 bars. The recapitulation is rounded off by a short presto, then prestissimo, section. In the latter the repeated minims of the first subject and the 'hallmark' of the second combine in a strong reminiscence of the Piano Concerto's opening, with typical imitational writing (see Ex. 41).

Rather more elaboration than is customary in Grieg's slow movements occur in the andante. It opens simply enough, however, with a tune closely related to the first phrase of the Homage March from *Sigurd Jorsalfar*. It is heard first on piano alone for eight bars, and then is taken up with particularly good effect by the 'cello above the piano's spread chords, with notable chromatic harmonisation of the second phrase (see Ex. 42). This leads to a middle section in F minor, then C sharp minor, in which the triplet of Ex. 42 is prominently and freely used. Ex. 42 does not return in its original simple setting but is played by the 'cello against reiterated triplet chords. It is interrupted by an impassioned reference to the middle section, on which also is based the very beautiful tranquillo coda. This is a finely designed and impressive movement which 'cellists could do worse than consider as a separate concert piece.

The same breadth and continuity of thought are lacking in the finale which contains many tedious sequential and repetitive passages. Only two points of interest need be mentioned. It opens with a mysterious quasi-recitative passage for 'cello only, which forms no part of the thematic material of the movement proper (or of any other movement) but is introduced again just before the recapitulation, and is hammered out, *fff*, at the end—a striking if enigmatic device. The other notable feature of the movement is that the second subject (Ex. 44) is an augmented, major variant of the A minor first subject (Ex. 43): a favourite device of Grieg's (cf. the Halling for male voice choir, Op. 30, No. 4; the *Norwegian Dance*, Op. 35, No. 3; the two cases in the *Symphonic Dances*, mentioned by Mr. Foss on p. 21; and Nos. 4 and 7 of the *Slåtter*, Op. 72).[1]

Grieg's only completed String Quartet, in G minor, Op. 27, was composed in 1877–8. In 1891 he wrote the first two movements, and left sketches for the other two, of a second Quartet, in F major. Julius Röntgen has asserted[2] that these two works present a strong contrast, the unfinished one being in classical quartet style, the G minor Quartet being less strict and more Norwegian. The form of the unfinished Quartet has certainly a ' classical ' appearance through its formal repeat of the exposition section in the first movement (only the early first Violin Sonata has a similar feature). In the G minor Quartet the form is cyclic and a seemingly unusual feature is that the slow motto-theme which introduces the first movement also serves, in a modified way, as its second subject. When one examines the theme, this innovation becomes less surprising, as will be seen in the paragraph below, and apart from it the first movement is not unconventional in form. The first movement of the unfinished Quartet also has a slow introductory motive which is employed prominently in the main body of the movement, and it is possible that, had Grieg completed the work, it would also have been cyclic in form. There is greater contrast between the two works in the actual quartet writing. The worst fault of the G minor Quartet,

[1] Though in all these cases major originals are afterwards played in augmentation in the minor, the reverse of the procedure in the Sonata.
[2] In *Die Musik*, Jahrgang VII, No. 5.

namely the overloading of the texture through simultaneous double-stopping in the four instruments, is eradicated in the later work, though there are still occasional orchestral thicknesses. Again the use of imitational writing is less oppressive in the unfinished Quartet, which is thus in some ways the more satisfactory of the two. The two movements were published posthumously by Julius Röntgen, and the miniature score[1] shows by comparison with the excerpts previously published in his *Die Musik* article, that he took it upon himself to ' improve ' what Grieg had already completed.

Apart from two weaknesses of the G minor Quartet mentioned above, it cannot be said that the use of a motto-theme throughout the work has the binding and unifying effect intended. The theme itself as it appears in the opening introduction is quoted as Ex. 45. It is the melody of one of Grieg's songs, *Spillemaend* (Fiddlers), Op. 25, No. 1. Note that the first three notes, G F D, are the Grieg melodic ' hall-mark ' in the less usual form with the seventh flattened (i.e. with F natural here instead of F sharp). That it should appear in every movement is not therefore surprising. In this opening movement it is easily transformed into the major to form the second subject (Ex. 46). The subject is quoted in full to show what is perhaps the most noticeable example, in the chamber music, of Grieg's melodic elaboration of a phrase of two or three notes, to which I have frequently alluded : bars 8–9, then 10–11 grow from the three notes of bars 6–7. Grieg clearly had more affection for this second subject than for the plodding first subject (Ex. 47) which shows marked similarity to that of the Piano Concerto's opening movement. But it lacks its rhythmic life, and the constantly imitational treatment becomes trying to the ear. Despite dull passages in the development there is more attempt than usual to interweave the two subjects. One of the more striking instances is quoted as Ex. 48 where an augmentation of the first subject embodies almost imperceptible suggestions of the second subject and of the motto-theme (i.e., the repeated minim D's of Ex. 45). This tranquillo passage occurs just before the recapitulation, which runs an orthodox course until, after a G.P., the key changes from G minor to G major and, with the three upper strings playing tremolo sul ponticello, the second subject is heard in augmentation on the 'cello. A brief presto based on a diminution of bars 1–3 of the motto-theme closes the movement; Professor Abraham has drawn attention in the Preface to the obvious influence of this passage on the parallel one in Debussy's Quartet.

---

[1] Peters-Eulenburg.

The most imaginative movement of the work follows, a Romance in ABABA form. The A section is a smooth andantino tune in B flat major; B is a contrasted allegro agitato in the tonic minor; A returns, still in B flat major, but in fresh setting and with a suggestion of the allegro agitato in the accompaniment; the B section reappears in a varied form in E flat minor with an interpolated four bars of A; which finally returns in yet another setting. The motto-theme, or rather the ' hall-mark ' therefrom, appears only and incidentally in the B section. In the third movement (Intermezzo), however, it is far more prominent and the use of the ' hall-mark ' begins to appear somewhat mechanical. Exs. 49 and 50 are instances, taken respectively from the opening and the coda of the movement, which is of scherzo type with a 2/4 middle section.

A few bars of the motto-theme, lento and treated imitationally, introduce the final presto al saltarello. If the material here is hardly memorable, the movement is not pulled together by an ' orchestral tutti ' statement of the motto-theme towards the end, or by the subsequent juxtaposition of brief suggestions of this theme and quotations from the third movement. One hesitates to apply the adjective ' cerebral ' to Grieg's music but in this case the device is a paper one, with no sense of musical necessity behind it. Far from giving unity to the movement, it makes its conclusion more disjointed than it needed to be.

Though Grieg may have intended the unfinished Quartet to be strictly ' classical ', in fact the form of its first movement is its weakest part. A slow introduction[1] precedes the allegro, which has an overlong exposition, formally repeated, a short development section, and a fairly exact recapitulation. Too many ideas are used up in the exposition, with the result that the major part of the development has to be provided by a laboured working of the introductory theme. Nevertheless the movement has striking passages and ideas. Rhythmic variety, so conspicuously absent in the first movement of the G minor Quartet, is gained by employing bars of 3/4 time in the midst of a basically 6/8 movement. The first instance of this (Ex. 51), appearing soon after the initial statement of the first subject, is also interesting for its two bars of whole-tone harmony. (I quote this passage as Grieg wrote it; comparison with p. 5 of the miniature score shows that Röntgen reversed the viola and 'cello parts in bars 1–3 and gave bar 4 entirely to second violin and viola.) Similarly

---

[1] In which Röntgen altered Grieg's three-note chords in the violin part to simple double-stops.

interesting is the stringendo (Ex. 52); but the building-up of this—
for Grieg—ambitious passage is punctured and collapses into the
simplest of second subjects. It is difficult for either the performer or
the listener to overlook the incongruity of styles, here and elsewhere,
in a movement by no means devoid of attractions.

The scherzo, a Norwegian springdans, also contains lively ideas,
especially rhythmical ideas. A typical example, occurring in the D
major middle section, is quoted as Ex. 53. (An almost exactly
similar theme appears in a piano piece, the *Albumblad*, Op. 28,
No. 4.) The cross-rhythm of the viola—2/4 against 3/4—shown here,
also figures in the opening D minor section, and thus characterises
the whole movement.

Earlier in this chapter, I suggested that the inspired writing to
be found in the Piano Concerto was largely due to the fact that Grieg
was here using the piano as a solo instrument; and that similar
inspiration is considerably less in evidence in the sonatas because he
was necessarily restricted in his use of the piano, having to match
it against a single stringed instrument of equal status. But why elect
to write duet sonatas? Grieg, with the example of Schumann before
him, must have realised that a greater number of strings would have
enabled him to use the piano with more freedom, and this in turn
would have given a stronger stimulus to his musical thought. Thinking of the Piano Concerto's qualities, and remembering that he
could write for strings, one feels that Grieg ought to have produced
a Piano Quartet or, better still, a Piano Quintet. Such a work might
well have been on a par with the Concerto. This is speculation :
the fact is that the only chamber music which Grieg left among his
unpublished manuscripts consists of two works, one an andante in
C minor for Piano Trio, dated 1878, the other (probably 1886) the
exposition of the first movement of a Piano Quintet in B flat major.
Had Grieg worked on the latter, would it have turned out to be his
masterpiece of chamber music? The reader may refer to the quotation of the beginning of the second subject (Ex. 54) and continue to
speculate.

5

The Piano Music

By

Kathleen Dale

THE PIANO WAS GRIEG'S chosen instrument. He played it from early childhood till the end of his life, and throughout the whole of his career he composed for it with enthusiasm and understanding. Of his seventy-four opus numbers, he devoted more than twenty to compositions for piano solo, a few to piano duets, and one to a work for two pianos; in addition, he arranged as piano solos and duets several of his own works which had originally been composed in another medium. Moreover, he designed the piano parts of his chamber music with particularly loving care, and the accompaniments to his songs with such exceptional felicity that they are a delight to all who have the good fortune to play them.

He was, indeed, a pianist's composer, yet his extensive output of works for piano solo is curiously unequal, both in the dimensions of the individual compositions and in their quality. He wrote only one large-scale work, the resplendent Concerto in A minor which, from its position of lonely grandeur, overshadows a whole host of small pieces, among which some are remarkable, many are delightful, others are trivial, and almost all are neglected—for reasons which will presently be discussed. Between these two extremes stand a couple of works of moderate proportions: the early Sonata, which, though it contains much attractive writing for the piano, is not sufficiently convincing as a whole work to attract the serious performer; and the somewhat later Ballade, a finely conceived set of variations whose pianistic layout and poetic character are calculated to appeal to the skilled and imaginative interpreter. It is consequently the only work bearing Grieg's name ever to appear in a piano-recitalist's programme.

That Grieg wrote so few long and so many short works is due to the fact that he was essentially a lyricist. Never robust in health, he lacked the necessary staying power to wrestle with the larger problems of form and balance. In the writing of miniatures, however, he found the ideal medium for the expression of his natural gifts.

When considering his works in the following pages it will be convenient to divide them into three categories: those, the most numerous, of small scale; those, very few, of larger dimensions; and those others which are pre-eminently nationalist in character. First, however, some of the possible causes for the present neglect of the shorter works will be briefly reviewed.

Few of Grieg's smaller piano pieces are really difficult to perform, and the great majority can be played by inexpert hands without undue effort. They are so eminently suitable as teaching pieces that they were early requisitioned for this purpose, consequently becoming the prey of young and inexperienced players and of unskilled amateurs, who performed them so frequently and so inadequately that all their freshness and charm were dulled, and listeners naturally wearied of them. What bad pianists had ruined in private, good pianists could hardly reinstate in public, and the ill-treated pieces lost their status in recital programmes. They were not designed primarily for concert purposes; but then, neither were many of Schumann's small pieces. Yet the latter have become an integral part of every recitalist's repertory, and it is in measuring the effectiveness of these little works of Schumann's that one can detect the shortcomings of Grieg's.

Where Schumann would generally group a set of pieces around a central poetic idea, and choose for each of them an appropriate key so as to create a coherent whole, Grieg, except in the *Holberg* Suite and in the *Scenes from Folk Life*, did neither. He seems to have pursued his ideas without any preconceived plan, and the ten books of *Lyric Pieces*, the sets of *Album Leaves, Humoresques, Poetic Tone Pictures*, and *Moods* give every sign of having been written with little regard to unity of style or affinity of key. This lack of planning may possibly be considered as denoting the freshness and irresistibility of his inspiration, but it hinders the ready acceptance of many sets of unrelated pieces. Few of the single items are strong enough to stand alone, and a large number are cast in a mould which is in itself unsatisfactory: episodical form, the normal proportions of which are destroyed by the exact repetition of both the middle and the recapitulatory sections. While this design is acceptable for short movements of classical type where emphasis falls on the formal balance, it is far less suitable for longer movements of impressionistic character in which continuity of outline is of greater importance.

These various disabilities of planning and of form, however, are of small account in comparison with the great beauty of Grieg's style, a beauty which is unique in its blending of a personal with a national idiom. His powers of portraying a scene or a mood, a landscape or a state of mind, and of surrounding a simple musical statement with an aura of enchantment are constantly exemplified in his works. That he gave poetic titles to almost every one of his piano solos indicates that he needed a definite image from which to develop his musical structure. Indeed, *all* Grieg's compositions, whether they bear titles or not, are evocative in character. Even when he wrote in sonata-form, for which activity he was temperamentally unsuited, picturesqueness was never very far away, and, in his longer works, many a radiant little contrasting interlude resembles a miniature, distant sunlit pasture seen through the open window of a sombre building, such as the early masters delighted to portray. That Grieg was himself a miniaturist, the short piano pieces most convincingly reveal.

The long series of these compositions begins at Op. 1 with a set of four movements: the only ones to appear without individual titles or a generic term. The composer sets out in tentatively Schumannesque style, as befits the dutiful eighteen-year-old Leipzig student, with a movement in D major strongly recalling his predecessor's *Novellette* in that key, but without any of its impetuosity. This was not the only time Grieg looked back to Schumann for guidance in weaving pianoforte texture. Countless instances could be cited; two must suffice here. From the right-hand part of the Alternativo of Schumann's Intermezzo, Op. 4, No. 6, he seems to have derived the right-hand figure at the beginning of the allegro capriccioso (variation 4) in the Ballade, Op. 24; and from the Impromptu, Op. 5, No. 8,[1] bars 9–10, he may have drawn support for his own many progressions of chords of the ninth. The second piece of Op. 1, in C major, shows the youthful Grieg taking his first steps as the arch-chromaticist he was later to become. The wistful movement bristles with accidentals to such an unwonted extent that even a practised Grieg player may be excused a few slips in sight-reading this otherwise not difficult score. The wayward middle section is of interest, not only in showing the composer feeling his way in the key of E minor (for which he was later to show a marked predilection), but also by the manner in which its capricious style foreshadows the scintillating passage of transition

---

[1] No. 8 of the second edition, though No. 9 of the first.

between the first and second subjects of the opening movement of the Concerto. The third piece, in A minor, is the first of the salon type which flowed only too readily from Grieg's pen : a graceful, well-mannered piece of indoor music presenting a striking contrast to its more rugged neighbour, the final movement in E minor. In the latter, the points of interest are the dark colouring, the varied metrical scheme which includes the lengthening of a four-bar phrase to six bars by means of a momentary, distant modulation—a chameleon-like change such as often adorned the pages of his later works (Ex. 55); a sequential passage prefiguring that in the Prelude of the *Holberg* Suite, and the appearance in the coda of the triplet figure with poignant harmony (Ex. 56) which became the motive of his *Lonely Wanderer*, Op. 43, No. 2, some years later.

The next collection, *Seks Poetiske Tonebilleder* (Poetic Pictures), Op. 3, opens and closes with movements in Grieg's favoured key, E minor, both pieces showing a surer command of keyboard style. The second movement, in B flat, is a warmly pulsating cantabile which conjures up visions of the future *Erotik*, Op. 43, No. 5, and the Canon in B flat minor, Op. 38, No. 8; the third, in C minor, is robust and purposeful, while the fourth, in A major, is full of subtle syncopations and suspensions, and despite the repetition of the alternating sections is a continuous and smoothly running whole piece. The remaining movement in F is the only one to which Grieg imparted a mildly northern flavour. It opens with an artless melody of folk-song type, and later on the bare fifths of the accompaniment lend a pastoral tinge to the scheme. It is a forerunner of the kind of piece which in later years Grieg would dignify by a distinctive Norwegian title.

Between the completion of Op. 3 and the composition of Op. 6, Grieg made the acquaintance in Copenhagen of his fellow-countryman, the composer Rikard Nordraak, who drew his attention to the wealth of Norwegian folk-music awaiting exploration. The meeting was of the utmost importance to Grieg, for it changed his whole musical outlook, and from that time onwards he lost no opportunity of utilising the treasury of native melody and rhythm. That he continued to produce compositions which evinced the strength of the German domination to which he had early been subject cannot be denied, but the Norwegian element in his work grew gradually stronger until it suffused his whole style with its northern lights. The part it played in enlarging his harmonic resource will be discussed later, and Mr. Horton has still more to say on Nordraak's influence in the concluding chapter of this book.[1]

The immediate result of the fresh stimulus was a set of four *Humoresker,* Op. 6, written in 1865 and dedicated to Nordraak. The somewhat inept title indicates that Grieg as yet lacked the courage of his new convictions, for he would not otherwise have hesitated to name the pieces ' Norwegian dances '.[2] Such, indeed, they are; three of them energetic, rhythmical and agreeably ' national '; the first and fourth of springdans type, and the second akin to a halling. It is the fourth which shows the greatest advance in pianoforte style and which points to some of the more elaborate writing in the Ballade, Op. 24. A chiaroscuro effect is produced by the alternate use of the high and low registers of the instrument; acciacature increase the feeling of tension; a rocking bass with a bare fifth on the weak beat lends grace; a mounting crescendo above a dominant pedal heightens the excitement of the coda which, though in the major mode, ends surprisingly with a rapidly ascending melodic minor scale resolving on a major triad. In contrast to these three lively dances, the remaining piece, in C major, allegretto con grazia, while equally blithe in spirit is tender in expression, its lilting rhythm presaging the haunting refrain of Solveig's song. The enchanting little coda is the first of the remote, dreamy type which Grieg often appended to his quieter pieces.

These early pieces have been considered in some detail because they bear within them seeds which came to fruition in many of the composer's later works. A pianist whose only acquaintance with Grieg has been made through the Concerto or the larger works might turn back to them to be refreshed by their youthful spontaneity and their morning-starriness.

The next of Grieg's smaller piano works, his Op. 12, is the first of the ten books of *Lyriske Stykker* (Lyric Pieces) which were written between 1867 and 1901 and comprise sixty-six pieces in all. The continuity of the series was occasionally interrupted by the composition of other short piano works, three of which, Op. 28, 37 and 40, will be touched upon here, out of chronological order, as will a few others later on under their appropriate category, so that the discussion of the *Lyric Pieces* may proceed unbroken.

---

[1] See p. 114.
[2] The opening two-bar motive of No. 2 is identical with the opening motive of a folk-song from Trondhjem, *Alle mann hadde fota* (Every man had a foot, mine had none).—ED.

Of the four *Albumblade* (Album Leaves), Op. 28, the first, a conventional salon piece, had been composed before the opening set of the *Lyric Pieces*: the others followed at intervals between 1874 and 1878. The second might have been composed upon hearing the First Act of *Tristan and Isolde*, so reminiscent is it of the languorous chromaticism therein. It does, however, contain a tiny interlude of pure Grieg: a sequence of decorative arpeggios on the chord of the ninth. The next piece is the first to be written in a style Grieg particularly favoured later on: the alternation of the polished with the pastoral, of the atmosphere of the salon with that of the sæter. It opens and closes as a graceful valse in A major, but the middle section flies away into A minor for a springdans in the mountains.

The last movement, likewise constructed in alternating sections, is different in character and is definitely Norwegian in colour all the way through, the only contrast being furnished by the opposing nostalgic and carefree moods of the sections. It is of similar type to the later, better-known *Lyric Pieces*, *Homesickness*, Op. 57, No. 6, and *Once upon a time*, Op. 71, No. 1.

The two Valses-Caprices for pianoforte duet, Op. 37 (which were also arranged for piano solo by the composer), are warmly expressive pieces, full of unusual harmonic progressions. The trio section of the second is composed of unbelievably slender material: an eight-bar phrase of two figures: one a block of four reiterated chords, the other the continuous alternation of a melody-note with the semitone below. The phrase is repeated nine times in succession, each time with only a slight, though delectable, change in the harmony or in the pitch of the melodic line. Far from being monotonous, the effect is magical, and the feeling of suspense as to where the next modulation will lead is not relaxed until the end of the ninth repetition, when the trio merges without break or hesitation into the recapitulation as though there had never been the slightest doubt of its ultimate destination.

The suite *Fra Holbergs Tid* (From Holberg's Time), Op. 40, must be mentioned here, for although it is infinitely better known in its orchestral version, it was originally written as a piano solo. It is an avowed pastiche, but since it was composed to commemorate an eighteenth-century personage, it could hardly have been more fitly devised to evoke the desired atmosphere of that period. In contemplating it one can only feel admiration for the composer who could thus set aside his own individuality, could write so ably and compellingly in a style poles apart from his own, and leave so few of his charming finger-prints upon the work produced.[1]

An adequate discussion of the complete collection of the *Lyric Pieces* would require far more space than is available in a single chapter dealing with the whole of Grieg's works for piano. The volume of 211 pages is a treasure-house of diverse and interesting exhibits and is so representative of Grieg's art as a whole that it would be a fascinating task to examine each piece separately. This being impossible here, an attempt will be made to classify the contents into a few distinct groups, and, by drawing particular attention to some of the pieces which typify the groups to which they belong, to give an idea of the nature of the whole series.

Up till 1867 Grieg had not applied descriptive titles to any of his single pieces, but from now onwards he gave a distinctive title to everything he wrote for the piano. Moreover, the titles he chose generally correspond so aptly to the musical content that they are in themselves something of a guide to the classification of the various kinds of movement to be found in the volume, which may be divided as follows: a large number of pieces of impressionistic character, a smaller number expressive of moods, and others of more abstract quality; to which may be added a few dances, both outdoor and indoor, a few sketches with a folk-tune outline, and a sprinkling of salon pieces. It need hardly be said that this classification does not claim to be more than tentative. Many of the pieces might be regarded as belonging to two or even more categories.

The impressionistic and subjective pieces, types which the composer had not yet attempted and which together number more than half the total, must receive the most attention since they represent the essential Grieg and display almost every facet of his personal style.

The impressionistic pieces start simply enough in Op. 12 with the *Watchman's Song*, which Grieg wrote after attending a performance of *Macbeth*. In the Peters edition of the *Lyric Pieces* it is prefaced by a note saying that it was Shakespeare's *Macbeth* which inspired the composition; on the other hand, Grieg's friend, Julius Röntgen, states in his book that it was *Schiller's* version of the drama, in which the translator replaced the porter's ribald soliloquy by a watchman's song:

> Verschwunden ist die finstre Nacht,
> Die Lerche schlägt, der Tag erwacht.

[1] Compare the opposite view expressed by Mr. Foss on p. 23.—ED.

51

Röntgen implies that Grieg based his melody upon the metre of this song, but it requires a considerable effort of imagination to fit the two together satisfactorily; moreover, nothing in Schiller's verse corresponds with the ' Intermezzo ' of mysterious pianissimo arpeggi and subdued fanfares which Grieg expressly marked ' Spirits of the Night '. It seems more reasonable to regard the whole piece as an evocation of the contrast between radiant day and eerie night described by the porter in his song. In this type of picturesque composition Grieg attained greater sureness of delineation with the quivering *Butterfly*—a moto perpetuo of fluttering semiquavers, the tragic *Lonely Wanderer*, the tremulous *Little Bird*, and the expectantly throbbing *To the Spring*, and reached a pinnacle of expressiveness in Op. 54 with the plaintive, Wagnerian *Shepherd Boy* and the ghostly, dream-like *Bell-Ringing*. The last-named is possibly the most truly impressionistic of any of Grieg's works, and probably his most original piano solo. With the exception of a few common chords in the closing bars and a couple of sixths and fourths at the first cadence, it is constructed entirely of fifths : bare fifths in the left hand on the strong beats, alternating with fifths which are often decorated by acciacature thirds in the right hand on the weak beats. With the sonority added by the pedal, the whole effect is one of confused vibrations suspended in the air, just as in Debussy's *Cathédrale engloutie* a similar sound, produced by different means, seems to be floating on the sea. The likeness between the two pieces is enhanced by the coincidence of their both being written in the key of C major.

The impressionistic pieces continue, still on a high level, with the portrait of Gade, Op. 57, No. 2, one of the composer's mentors in his earlier years. This piece is the very antithesis of the one just described, for it is a model of conventionality and is hardly impressionistic at all. It is included in this group because it conveys a very clear impression of the Danish composer it portrays, showing him to have been mildly impulsive, earnest and warm-hearted. Numerous sequences of canonic imitations supported by a throbbing accompaniment lend the piece a suitably academic tinge without detracting from its spontaneity. To a slightly later period belongs *The Brook*, Op. 62, No. 4. The frequent changes in the harmonies and the many breaks in the restless semiquaver figuration denote that this is no placidly flowing stream, but a headstrong rill such as leaps and bounds down the sheer slopes of the Norwegian hills. The type of piano writing points forward to the accompaniment of the song *Ved Gjaetle-bekken* (At the Brook), Op. 67, No. 8, which Grieg composed a few years later. In the next piece, *Phantom*, the quality of evanescence is conveyed by a series of rapid modulations during the course of which the principal phrase drifts unchanged through keys successively a semitone below that of the first statement : a bold procedure, which is, however, justified by the exigencies of the fantastic situation. Still later comes *Evening in the mountains*, Op. 68, No. 4, and by this time (1898) Grieg's skill in tone-painting was highly developed. This E minor piece in 2/4 time, though delicate in character, is boldly conceived; Mr. Foss has already discussed the later version for small orchestra.[1] Between a lightly sketched introduction of seven bars and a coda of six, two different versions of the same material are presented; the first, an intensely expressive single-line melody for the right hand (Ex. 10), thirty-eight bars in length, coming to an expectant pause on the dominant; the second, an exact repetition of this melody, now richly harmonised until it dies away above a tonic pedal preceding the coda. The remarkable feature of the piece is that each of the strongly contrasted sections is sufficiently convincing in its own way to make it difficult to decide which of the two is the more successful—the unharmonised or the harmonised.

The last of the impressionistic pieces that need be mentioned here is *Summer Evening*, Op. 71, No. 2. This tranquil two-page sketch is the only one of all Grieg's piano solos to be written in D flat major, and, strangely enough, it displays a stronger affinity in style than any other of his solo pieces to the slow movement of the Concerto, which is also written in this key. Both works are instinct with the lucent serenity and expansiveness which characterise the Norwegian summer evening scene. The means employed to create the quietly glowing atmosphere are not at all exceptional. A few chords of the ninth, eleventh and thirteenth resolving unexpectedly; a few modulating sequences proceeding upwards by step of a semitone; and a few descending semiquaver passages of broken fourths above spread chords of the seventh are the only special harmonic devices employed. The choice of register and the spacing of chords on the keyboard, however, cause a magical lightness and clarity to pervade the whole piece, the little corruscating semiquaver passages intensifying rather than disturbing the tranquillity, as do also the decorative scale-passages in the adagio of the Concerto. It sounds almost as though the composer had turned back thirty years and

[1] See p. 22.

recaptured part of the spirit which inspired his greatest piano work.

Among the pieces expressing a variety of moods, the sombre outnumber the sunny. Of the two entitled *Melancholy*, the first, Op. 47, No. 5, is essentially in Grieg's early, Schumannesque manner, while the second, Op. 65, No. 3, exemplifies his later, more rugged personal style and is the more interesting pianistically on account of excursions into the very lowest depths of the keyboard. In wistful mood, too, is *Homesickness*, Op. 57, No. 6, with its nostalgic first and last sections in E minor, separated by the gracious little episode in E major affording a glimpse of the longed-for homeland. Among the happiest pieces in this genre are *Gratitude* (more correctly, *Thanks*), Op. 62, No. 2, and *At the Cradle*, Op. 68, No. 5. In the first-named, a long, well-sustained diatonic melody, followed by a little figure rising eagerly by chromatic sequence, expresses such an exuberance of feeling that it makes the impression of the composer's being almost overwhelmed by the depth of his own gratitude. In the last few bars the little figure descends calmly over a tonic pedal to a solemn plagal cadence : a fitting conclusion to this pæan of thanksgiving. *At the Cradle* is as serene as the preceding piece is impassioned, and is instinct with the whole-hearted freshness which was noted in the composer's early works, with the difference that by now chromaticism has become an integral part of the construction instead of being an extraneous element. As regards form, too, the piece is more satisfactory than many of its fellows, for it dispenses with the exact repetition of the opening section after the contrasting episode, and recalls rather than restates the principal thematic material, eventually relegating the melody to the left hand which then allows it to fade away beneath the right-hand harmonies.

Among the movements of more abstract type, two bearing the non-committal title of *Melody*, belonging to Op. 38 and Op. 47 respectively, present several points of interest, especially in their strong mutual contrast. The first is a docile, rather uneventful little sketch in C major, in which a pungent discord—an augmented second clashing with the chromatic semitone immediately above it—makes an occasional, surprising appearance in a prominent position, and in which all the phrases are of uneven length, either seven or nine bars—a rare occurrence in Grieg's usually square-cut structures. The second, in A minor, written in 6/8 time and in unbroken trochaic metre from beginning to end, is dark in colour and restless in character. Within an entirely regular rhythmical scheme it canters in determined fashion through a succession of keys, returning to the starting-point to go through the whole procedure a second time before the tension is relaxed, the pace of the canter slackens and the movement is brought to a final, uneasy standstill in the lower regions of the keyboard.

Of the remaining, less numerous categories of the *Lyric Pieces*, one example of each must suffice to indicate their style. Typical of the outdoor dances is the C major Halling, Op. 71, No. 5, a boisterous movement which starts off with a sudden tuning-up of instruments followed by an expectant silence, and then settles down to a succession of strongly accented tunes, the first of which is almost identical in outline with that of the *Norwegian Bridal Procession*, Op. 19. The tunes are accompanied by lively, decorated pedal basses, entailing constant wide leaps by the left hand, sometimes more than an octave in extent. The effect is one of hard brilliance, and almost of virtuosity too, for Grieg allows himself the only glissando of his career. The most characteristic of the indoor dances is the *Valse-Impromptu*, Op. 47, No. 1, a movement actually in E minor although it opens in the key of A minor, as if the composer were still haunted by his recently re-scored *Anitra's Dance* (cf. Ex. 101). The melody and the bass proceed by similar motion almost all the way through, and as their main direction is nearly always downwards, the prevailing mood is somewhat chastened. Only one principal melodic theme is used, and in the contrasting episode in B minor it is entrusted for a time to the left hand, which treats it as an expressive solo beneath light right-hand chords before allowing it to come running up the keyboard by arpeggio to resume its original dominant position in the uppermost part. The piece is particularly well written for the pianist, many of the passages being finely adjusted between the two hands.

Among the several pieces with a folk-tune outline, the Ballade in C minor, Op. 65, No. 4, is a shining example of the skilful treatment of a rather undistinguished melody. Grieg eschewed his customary chromaticisms and placed the tune in a setting of remarkable simplicity. The eight-bar phrase is repeated six times, each time with some slight variation, either in pitch, key, dynamic marking, doubling of the melody or fullness of harmony, and at the end of the piece the listener is left with the feeling of having heard a pleasantly monotonous old ballad sung with deep conviction by an ancient bard.

As an example of the salon genre, the piece bearing that very title,

Salon, Op. 65, No. 4, should be the most appropriate choice. It is written in A major, but like the earlier *Butterfly*, opens with a broken chord of the dominant ninth, after which it does not definitely establish its tonality until the fifteenth bar. Thence, having at last achieved a perfect cadence, it immediately makes a short expedition into A flat, soon to return enharmonically to the tonic key. The lively metrical scheme, which alternates between 6/8 and implied 3/4 time, adds lightness to this very graceful little piece.

Grieg's last set of piano pieces, Op. 73, composed in 1906, although entitled *Stemninger* (Moods), is really a continuation of the *Lyric Pieces* with their wide variety of style. Only the first, *Resignation*, can be considered as portraying a definite mood. This is the composer's swan-song in the key of E minor and is a short, concentrated movement of prelude type, built upon a single phrase which is developed to a telling climax and reduced to its simplest terms to form the coda. The next piece, a Scherzo-Impromptu in B flat, is lively, capricious, and as expansive as the previous piece is terse. In construction it is of similar character to the Valse-Impromptu, Op. 47, No. 1, but it is more sprightly, and pianistically more interesting and effective on account of its crisp ornaments and exciting stretto passages. It is followed by *Nocturnal Ride* in D minor, an eight-page movement which, though metrically interesting in some of its details, lacks conviction as a whole, and conveys the impression of a ride far less strongly than does the cantering *Melody* of Op. 47. The succeeding piece, only a page in length, is a genuine folk-tune from the Valders region of Norway, set with extreme simplicity and aptness above a gently rocking accompaniment based upon alternate tonic and dominant pedals, which make way at the end for an extended plagal cadence. The fifth movement, a Study in F minor bearing the sub-title *Hommage à Chopin*, is a pastiche as successful in its romantic style as is any movement of the *Holberg* Suite in the classical manner. Once again, Grieg effaced himself and proved that he could master a style alien to his own, and this time the task seems to have been a particularly congenial one. In the *Students' Serenade* which follows, Grieg is his Norwegian self again, weaving an artless web of melody in 6/8[1] time above a texture of chromatic harmonies within independently moving inner and lower threads; the *Serenade* is restrained in tone as though the students were paying homage to an old and revered professor. With the final

---

[1] Was not this melody one of the sources of Delius's *On hearing the first cuckoo in spring*, as the folk-tune of Grieg's Op. 66, No. 14, was admittedly the other?—ED.

movement, *Mountaineer's Song* in G minor, Grieg takes his farewell as an impressionist composer, leaving behind him a last idealised picture of his native scene. The short refrain of the mountaineer's song is stated in different keys and at different pitches, is placed above long-held basses of fifths, and chased by echoing canons until the volume of tone gradually amassed seems to reverberate around the mountain-tops before eventually dying away into the stillness of vast spaces. It is a touching farewell, and most satisfying as a pianist's last word. It is therefore much to be regretted that its position should be challenged by the posthumous publication in 1908 of three piano solos, none of which bears comparison with any of Op. 73, and which together add nothing to Grieg's reputation. The first, *Wild Dance* (undated), and the third, *Tempest Clouds* (1891), which was left unfinished and had to be completed by its editor, Julius Röntgen, are diffuse, incondite pieces of music; but the third, *Procession of Gnomes* (1898), a concise little movement in a vein which Grieg was inclined to overwork, presents an interesting point to musicians who look for similarities in the music of Grieg and Debussy. Written in 2/4 time, the piece is crisp and regular throughout, with hardly a break in the metre of two quavers and one crotchet in every bar, until suddenly, a few bars before the end, this scheme gives way to a totally unexpected succession of common chords in root position descending deliberately from the top of the keyboard at the rate of two to each bar, gradually slowing down to one a bar on the weak beat till it disappears on meeting the metrical figure, now a pianissimo shadow of its former self, at the other extremity of the keyboard. This ethereal passage is truly Debussyan, and brings to mind the opening of *Danse sacrée*, composed in 1904.

In the composition of larger works Grieg was less at ease than with miniatures, for his musical ideas were nearly always of diminutive size, and when he wished to create a work of any length he had few resources beyond that of inventing a succession of short, well-defined phrases and of repeating them whenever it was necessary to fill in time and space. Consequently, his works in sonata-form, delightful as they are in respect of their ever-fresh and poetic material, are fragmentary instead of coherent in plan, graphic rather than architectonic in style. This is especially true of his solitary, early Piano Sonata in E minor, Op. 7, his first essay in this form. The opening and closing movements, both in sonata-form, give the impression that the composer is constantly harassed by formal conventions though determined to follow them; in the second movement he subjects the slight material to a strain rather greater than it can bear, and only in the minuet-and-trio does he seem to be on surer ground and able to move with perfect ease within necessarily narrower confines. This movement, with its rugged minore opening and conclusion and its pastoral maggiore, is of the same type as many of the *Lyric Pieces* and others already mentioned. The whole Sonata is written in a convincingly pianistic style, but it gives few hints of the coming splendour of the Concerto.

By the time Grieg wrote this later work, his Op. 16, he had already composed two violin sonatas, and it may have been the additional experience thus gained, and perhaps the assistance afforded him by the availability of orchestral colouring and contrast, which enabled him to produce a large-scale work of far more satisfying proportions than heretofore. He had, too, begun to assimilate the essence of his native folk-song, as is evidenced by the thematic material and melodic outline of all three movements. The whole work is as attractive on account of the fresh Norwegian colouring as it is by reason of the artistically controlled brilliance of the solo part.

In the next important piano composition, the Ballade, Op. 24, Grieg discovered himself as a writer of variations: a form which must have appealed strongly to him in that it provided an ideal medium for the practice of his lyrical gifts. In style and texture some of the individual variations are of similar character to the best of his miniatures, but they have the greater advantage of being unified by a definite theme, so that as they proceed they gather a momentum denied to sets of unrelated pieces. In the interval between the completion of the Concerto and the composition of the Ballade, Grieg had learned to know Liszt, who showed great interest in his work and gave him much encouragement. It might therefore have been expected that the Ballade would show the influence of Liszt's style, and it is surely a proof of Grieg's artistic integrity that he did not succumb to the blandishment of Lisztian virtuosity, but continued to develop his own individual manner. Virtuosity seldom entered into Grieg's scheme, and passages of that variety of meretricious dexterity which Sir Donald Tovey so aptly, if disrespectfully, described as 'Liszt's glass-chandelier pianistics', are blessedly absent from his work. In the Ballade, Grieg displayed several aspects of pianistic style over and above those he had manifested in the Concerto, and the work is remarkable both for its brilliance and its depth.

The theme is a folk-song from Nordland, *E kann so mangen ein vakker sang,*[1] sixteen bars in triple time in the minor mode of G, taken (like so many others) from Lindeman's collection and it is instructive to compare Grieg's more sophisticated harmonisation with Lindeman's (Ex. 57). The theme is immediately arresting by reason of its inherent melancholy, its limited melodic range and threefold repetition of the opening phrase, its alternations in tonality between tonic minor and relative major, and its subdued chromatic harmonies determined by the stepwise descending bass. There are fourteen variations, in the first eight of which the theme is preserved almost intact either melodically or harmonically, though it is subjected to such elaborate metamorphosis that player and listener are as keenly aware of the intrinsically beautiful piano-writing as of the skill with which the theme is varied.

In the first variation the chromatic harmonies emerge from the solidified state of their presentation to melt gently into flowing triplets, and in the following, allegro agitato, the time changes into 9/8 to allow six busy semiquavers to stir each beat into activity. The third, adagio 3/4, is a tranquil duo; through a tunnel of semiquavers formed by the extreme parts, the theme threads its quiet way in the tenor part, throwing its reflection upwards a major third into the alto part so that the harmonies of tonic minor and relative major run concurrently for a time—a kind of polytonality Grieg often employed. The sprightly fourth variation, allegro capriccioso, is decorated by pleasantly pungent chromatic semitones, while the fifth—the first double-variation—consists mainly of passages of impassioned recitative counter-balanced by unperturbed cadential corollaries.

The next two variations are closely related. In the first, allegro scherzando, every beat is broken up into a dotted figure in double notes, each hand playing the same material an octave distant and a beat apart from each other. In the second, this scheme is liquefied,

[1] I suggest that the words, of which I give a rough translation, may have lent the melody a special significance in Grieg's eyes:

I know so many a pretty song
Of foreign parts far away-o,
But never once have I heard them sing
Of what we see every day-o.

And so I'm going for to try my hand
And make a tune so they'll understand
It's fine up here in our Northern land,
Though Southern folks may not say so.

Did he not see in the sturdy 'Nordland yeoman' something of himself?—ED.

so to speak, by being presented entirely in running semiquavers, still at an octave's distance, but now only a semiquaver apart and in strict canon throughout except for a very brief interruption. Then gaiety gives way to grief, and the eighth variation, lento, might serve as the accompaniment to a solemn procession. Heavy chords on the strong beats are echoed throughout by single notes, or octaves high above and deep below, on the weak beats, and during the short middle section the harmonic texture is punctuated by an upper and lower dominant pedal sounding like the tolling of a bell.

The ninth variation, un poco andante, marks the transition to a more symphonic type of composition, and is different from all the others in being the only one which, while referring to the theme, transcends its melodic and structural boundaries and is in itself a complete and independent piece of music. It is the most characteristic, too, of Grieg's lyrical style, the dreaming cadenzas based upon the chord of the ninth on the flattened supertonic, as well as the canonic imitation at the cadences, marking it unmistakably as his own.

The remaining variations are less concentrated in expression, and more elaborate in piano technique. They are no longer separate pieces, but form one continuous stream of music. The tenth, un poco allegro e alla burla, is a lively yet graceful dance in 12/8 time, ending with a tense crescendo of spread diminished-seventh chords mounting by semitones to reach the dominant of D. Instead, however, of proceeding to this key for the next variation, più animato, the music suddenly drops five octaves below to a pianissimo decorated dominant pedal in the unexpected key of D *flat*. There it remains murmuring uneasily for five bars before retracing its steps towards the original tonality, travelling by way of keys successively a minor third above each other : one of Grieg's favourite progressions. This section, the eleventh variation, is in the nature of a transition rather than being an independent movement, the shifting tonality making it an effective prelude to its triumphant successor in the tonic major, meno allegro e maestoso, which glitters with double octaves and whose swirling cadenza links it to the thirteenth variation, allegro furioso. The minor mode is resumed, and fury is graphically expressed by spread chords pulling fiercely away from each other in contrary motion. At the end, the feeling of antagonism is heightened by a violent altercation between the major triad on the dominant and that on the flattened leading-note. The dominant emerges victorious, and thus prepares the way for the last variation, prestissimo, a short but determined hammering-in of the chief phrase of the theme, clinched by repeated canonic imitations and then sharply halted by a dramatic plunge to a low, bare submediant octave. After an impressive pause, a final pianissimo statement of the main substance of the theme brings the work to a peaceful close. Heard once more in its native simplicity, and considered in retrospect, the folk-song sounds even sadder, even more expressive and infinitely more venerable than at its first unfolding, when its melancholy beauty had still to be enhanced by all the wealth of artistry which the composer was to bestow upon it.

Grieg's only other keyboard composition of similar dimensions was another set of variations, the *Old Norwegian Melody*, Op. 51, this time for two pianos, and like its predecessor, based upon a Norwegian folk-song, the ballad of *Sjugur å Trollbrura* (Sigurd and the Troll-Bride), beginning : ' A kungjen han sto på högelofts svol ' (Ex. 98) which he had already arranged simply for piano as No. 4 of his *Seks Norske Fjeldmelodier* (Six Norwegian Mountain Melodies). That it is the less successful of the two sets of variations may be due to the fact that the composer, employing four hands instead of two, was tempted to concentrate his thought more upon the volume and diversity of tone they could produce than upon the quality of the music they might express. He afterwards orchestrated the work, omitting the tenth and twelfth variations and making cuts in the finale.

The nationalist tendencies in Grieg's art have been noted in passing, but the piano works to which he devoted his strongest nationalist sympathies have yet to be surveyed. They are seven in number, three of them being original works based upon folk-tunes, either authentic or idealised, while the remaining four are sets of arrangements of folk-tunes.

Of the first-named, the earliest is *Folkelivsbilleder* (Scenes from Folk Life), Op. 19, a set of three movements which are linked together by key-relationship and by mutual thematic cross-reference. The second movement is the well-known *Norwegian Bridal Procession passing by*, a piece of exceptionally sensitive piano-writing which takes a high place among Grieg's miniature tone-poems. The *Improvisata upon two Norwegian Folk-tunes*, Op. 29, are less satisfactory, for they lack the impulsiveness which distinguishes the movements of Op. 19. Nevertheless, the animated trio of the second, on the song *Dæ va eigong en Kungje*, attracts attention by the deftness of the piano-writing and by the little wisps

of alluring chromaticisms which float across the scene, suggesting
that the composer must have had the 'Venusberg' music in mind
at the time of sketching it. The first is based on the dialogue
song *Guten å Gjenta på fjöshjellen* (The boy and girl in the
cow-barn); comparison with the simple arrangement of the tune
in the set of *Six Norwegian Mountain Melodies* shows that the
allegro section (the girl's reply) is a distortion in 6/8 of an original
in 3/4. The well-known *Norwegian Dances*, Op. 35, for piano
duet (arranged by the composer also for piano solo) are, however,
delightfully full of conviction, the attractive thematic material being
submitted to such sympathetic treatment that the pieces are far
more genuinely Norwegian in flavour than the rather half-hearted
Improvisata. They demonstrate how thoroughly the composer had
by that time absorbed the native idiom into his own. Like most
of the folk-tunes used in works earlier than Op. 66, the themes are
practically all borrowed from Lindeman's *Norske Fjeldmelodier*; the
only original theme is that of the introduction and poco meno mosso
of No. 4. (The main theme of No. 4 is a halling from Hallingdal.)
In No. 3, another halling, Grieg preserves not only Lindeman's key—
as he usually does—but, unusually, Lindeman's harmonisation of
the first four bars. Mention has already been made earlier in this
book[1] of Grieg's habit of basing a contrasting middle section on his
main theme by lengthening its note-values and changing its mode,
as he does here in No. 3. In No. 2, yet another halling (from Aamot),
he bases his middle section, allegro, on part of the main allegretto
tranquillo but (exceptionally) in the *relative* minor. In No. 1, *Sinklars Marsch*, the cantabile middle section is simply the trio of the
original march with doubled note-values. *Sinclair's March*, incidentally, like the song, *Sinklar drog over salten hav*, commemorates the
destruction of a force of Scottish volunteers for the Swedish army
during the Thirty Years' War.

The four sets of folk-tune arrangements (Opp. 17, 66 and 72, and
the little set of *Seks Fjeldmelodier* without opus number), are of
exceptional interest to students of Grieg's art, inasmuch as they
show, firstly, the nature of the material to which he so often turned
for inspiration and upon which he based orchestral, choral and
chamber as well as keyboard works; secondly, the manner in which
he treated it and enriched it from his own harmonic resources; and
thirdly, the influence it exerted upon the formation of his personal
style. To read these little pieces is like perusing the pages of a

[1] See pp. 21 and 41.

thesaurus of Griegian chords and phrases, or delving into a dictionary of familiar quotations from his works. It is difficult, indeed, to imagine these folk-tunes without Grieg's settings, so appropriate do they appear; or, on looking back over his art as a whole, to think of his original compositions without the folk-song background, so inseparably are they interwoven and so closely do some of the distinguishing features of Norwegian folk-music correspond with some of his stylistic idiosyncrasies.

Among the most characteristic of the folk-song traits are : a fall of a step of one degree followed by a falling interval of a third; a succession of thirds either ascending or descending; the hovering of a melody around one note, and the frequent repetition of a short phrase or figure. Even a slight acquaintance with Grieg's work suffices to identify these traits as they are embodied in the texture of a few of his best-known compositions. For instance, the first is the ' hallmark ' pointed out by Mr. Foss and Mr. Frank; the second trait may be seen in the allegretto of the Violin Sonata in F and in the C major *Humoresque* for piano. The third occurs in the refrain of Solveig's song, and the fourth in any of the movements of the first *Peer Gynt* Suite. These examples comprise only a fraction of the countless numbers to be found throughout Grieg's works.

The first of the four sets of folk-tune arrangements is *Norske danser og viser* (Norwegian Dances and Folk-songs), Op. 17, containing twenty-five tunes from Lindeman's collection which Grieg had just discovered,[1] only four of which are more than one page in length, and the remainder are miniatures varying from three lines to a page. One of Grieg's methods of treating the material was to prefix a brief introduction to the tune for the purpose of establishing the style of the accompaniment, and then to present it several times in succession, each time with a variation in the harmony or figuration. He generally appended a few bars as a coda. This was the manner in which he usually treated the dances, but in the songs he seldom repeated the tune more than twice, and sometimes he stated it only once. Of the pieces in Op. 17, the Springdans, No. 1, shows his capacity for imparting diversity to several successive repetitions of a tune; No. 4, *Niels Tallefjoren*, the pensive charm with which he could invest a single statement of a melody; and No. 6, *Bridal Song*, his skill in adding a coda to correspond in style with his setting of a delightful twelve-bar tune. In this volume may be found the tunes, *Saag du nokke kjæringa mi* and *Brulåt* (Bridal Song) (Nos. 23

[1] No. 9 is given in Lindeman's *Koralbog* (Chorale Book).

and 24), which Grieg used later as the basis of each of the two contrasting sections in his fourth *Symphonic Dance* for orchestra, Op. 64, and it may be observed how simply he arranged the tunes for the piano, but how elaborately he developed them for the orchestra. Nos. 22 and 18 were also used in the second of the *Norwegian Melodies* for string orchestra, Op. 63. Similar later borrowings from the much less known—indeed almost unknown—set of *Seks norske fjeldmelodier* (Six Norwegian Mountain Melodies) have already been mentioned. These six arrangements are simple in texture, technically easy, and attractive, but of very slight importance.

The next volume, *Norske folkeviser* (Norwegian Folk Tunes), Op. 66, collected by Grieg himself, is much later in date and rather different in character, for it contains a higher proportion of longer pieces, in which the tunes are given a more colourful setting. Among the nineteen items, three are merely brief snatches of melody such as are sounded to call cattle back to the fold. One of these call-notes, No. 6, is used to form the prelude and postlude to a separate tune, but the other two are extended by the addition of ornaments and are subjected to changes of time and harmonisation until each is transformed into a complete miniature of charming, far-away character. The type of harmony Grieg employed in Op. 66 is even more strongly chromatic in flavour than that in Op. 17—the *Mountain Melodies* are more diatonic—and some of the chords and progressions would doubtless grate upon the ear of the folk-song purist. Nevertheless, considering the fundamentally sombre and monotonous character of Norwegian folk-songs, it may perhaps be conceded that Grieg's chromatic treatment tends to banish their sadness and to enhance their haunting attractiveness.

Of all the pieces in the two collections, the loveliest is *I Ola-Dalom, i Ola-Kjönn* (In Ola Dale), No. 14 of Op. 66. The tune is the one which Delius was later to use in *On hearing the first cuckoo in spring*, and in this setting of Grieg's the harmony is almost as Delian as that of Delius himself. The melody is treated strophically, and an interlude between each verse determines the style of accompaniment for the next. In the first verse, the theme, which is in 6/8 time, is placed in the top voice, with simple harmonies incorporating the flattened leading-note, above a pedal bass of fifths alternately an octave apart, and always on the weak beats of the bar (Ex. 58). In the second, the melody pursues its interior way between a descending bass and a gently pulsating treble to reach a climax succeeded by a few bars which, in their rich, changing harmonies below an almost stationary melody, recall the trio of the second Valse-Caprice already described. In the last verse, the theme returns to the upper voice to be harmonised with many varieties of chords of the seventh until it evanesces into a decorated plagal cadence and a pianissimo tremolo in the heights of the keyboard.

Another very remarkable piece in the same book is No. 18, *Jeg går i tusind Tanker* (In deepest thought I wander), the most purely pianistic as well as the longest in the two collections. It occupies about four minutes in performance, and comprises three versions of a flowing sixteen-bar tune. Each statement is increasingly more elaborate and more extended than its predecessor, and the piano-writing becomes as decorative as that in some of the variations of the Ballade, although the harmonic scheme is less chromatic—indeed, it is rather unusually diatonic for late Grieg. The piece is marked andante religioso, and is characterised by the same fervour and sincerity which radiate from Grieg's last opus (74), the amazingly original *Four Psalms* for unaccompanied choir. If *In Ola Dale* may be described as a pastel, *Jeg går i tusind Tanker* might be likened to a stained-glass window, so warmly does it glow.

No. 19, *Gjendine's Lullaby*, which Grieg recorded from the singing of the girl Gjendine Slålien herself,[1] gives us one of our rare opportunities to study Grieg's second thoughts—thanks to the facsimile of his original harmonisation given in Yvonne Rokseth's *Grieg*.[2] Among the afterthoughts are the C sharp appoggiature in bars 4 and 8, and other changes may be noted in bars 9–13 (*a*) in the original harmonisation, and (*b*) as published (Ex. 59).

The last of the works of nationalist character, the *Slåtter*, Op. 72, is of quite another type, for in this collection Grieg made use of peasant material at second-hand, by transforming into full-sized piano pieces some of the traditional dance-music for Hardanger fiddle which had been noted down and adapted for solo violin by Johan Halvorsen. Grieg undertook the work at the request of Knut Dale, a fiddler from Telemarken, who had written to him in 1901 inviting his assistance in the preservation of this unique heritage of folk-music which was then in danger of disappearing. Grieg responded by making plans for Halvorsen to note down the tunes from Knut Dale's playing, and to send them to him to transcribe for piano. His letters to Halvorsen at this time bear witness to his own delight

---

[1] Gjendine's goat-horn with its three notes—E, F sharp, G—also gave him the opening motive of *Homesickness*, Op. 57, No. 6.

[2] Paris, 1933.

in the wild beauty of the tunes and their wealth of ornamentation; to his desire to give them suitable permanent form, and to his difficulties in arranging material which was so sensitive that it was, as he said, all too easy to destroy its fragrance. The dance-tunes themselves are subtle, vigorous and exultant : the very type of music which the hardy and intelligent peasantry of the Hardanger region would inevitably evolve for performance on their native fiddle, an instrument which differs from the violin in being furnished with a set of sympathetically vibrating strings. The inherently elaborate metrical scheme of the tunes is further complicated by the concurrent use of 6/8 and 3/4 time, and the frequent use of the sharpened fourth of the scale causes additional difficulties in harmonisation.[1] From a pianist's point of view the material appears utterly intractable, and the masterly way in which Grieg surmounted the many obstacles in adapting it for his own instrument can be truly appreciated only by closely comparing the piano transcriptions with Halvorsen's original notation for the violin (see Exs. 60 and 61).[2]

Grieg reproduced every possible feature of the uncouth wildness of the dances themselves, as well as of the rustic quality of the native instrument, by means of adding heavy accompanying bass-parts, by the frequent use of the cruder intervals, by wide spacing between the upper and lower parts, by crashing diatonic discords, incisive accents and ornaments, and by terse codas which clinch the argument. In two of the dances, Nos. 4 and 7, he introduced his favourite device of contrasting sections in the tonic minor, with the original material in augmentation. Elsewhere he kept strictly to the originals.

As a composer for the piano Grieg added little to keyboard technique, and his compositions owe their strongly individual style far more to his highly characteristic harmonic sense than to any specially original pianistic method of treating the material. There are, however, certain features which distinguish his piano-writing, among which are the following :

(*a*) The skilful employment of ornaments, principally mordents and acciacature, as an integral part of the texture, examples of which may be seen throughout the *Slåtter*, Op. 72, the *Scenes from Folk Life*, Op. 19, and in *Bell-ringing*, Op. 54, No. 6, and Valse-Impromptu, Op. 47, No. 1.

[1] Though, as Mr. John Horton shows in a later chapter (p. 122), these very difficulties were turned strikingly to account.—Ed.

[2] For a more detailed study of the *Slåtter*, see Mr. Horton's article in *Music and Letters*, October 1945.

(*b*) The use of a broken chord of the seventh or ninth, either as an undulating accompaniment to a melody, as in the *Notturno*, Op. 54, No. 4, bars 15–32; in the first movement of the Concerto, bars 44–48, and throughout the F major episode in the third movement; or as the basis for a passage of cloudy resonance controlled by the sustaining pedal, as in the slow movement of the Piano Sonata, bars 19–20; in the first movement of the 'Cello Sonata, bars 18–21, or in *At the Cradle*, Op. 68, No. 5, bars 23–27.

(*c*) The frequent repetition of a figure or phrase at widely different pitches, often at the distance of an octave and three times in succession, as in the first and last sections of the Scherzo, Op. 54, No. 5, throughout the Halling, Op. 38, No. 4, and in the *Slåtter*, No. 2, bars 23–29, 51–57, and 81–87.

(*d*) A long-sustained pedal bass beneath constantly changing harmonies, as in the opening section and bars 51–56 of the *Berceuse*, Op. 38, No. 1, in *At the Cradle*, Op. 68, No. 5, bars 1–4 and 32–37, and throughout the whole of the Halling, Op. 47, No. 4; or a continuous pedal-figure such as occurs in the third movement of the Violin Sonata in C minor, Op. 45, bars 21–42 and elsewhere in this movement, as well as in the middle section of *To the Spring*, Op. 43, No. 6, bars 45–56, and in the first movement of the 'Cello Sonata, where twelve bars over a stationary pedal are followed by sixteen bars above a flowing pedal-figure, bars 228–255.

(*e*) A single chord pulsating below an elaborate right-hand passage, as in the first movement of the Concerto, bars 68–70, and in *On the Mountains*, Op. 19, No. 1, bars 64–65; or two alternating chords performing the same function, as in the first movement of the 'Cello Sonata, bars 205–221.

(*f*) A line of expressive recitative in contrast to a tense harmonic situation, as in the Valse, Op. 38, No. 7, bars 33–37, *Album Leaf*, Op. 47, No. 2, bars 40–49, *Elegy*, Op. 47, No. 7, bars 35–38, and *Secret*, Op. 57, No. 4, bars 30–39.

(*g*) A quiet presentation of the opening theme in single octaves divided between the two hands, as at the beginnings of the second movement of the Violin Sonata in F, of *On the Mountains*, Op. 19, No. 1, of Nos. 16 and 17 of the *Folk-songs*, Op. 17, and of the song, *The Princess*.

(*h*) A single silent beat, or a whole silent bar following a telling phrase to allow it to make a deeper impression, as in *Resignation*, Op. 73, No. 1, and the *Humoresque*, Op. 6, No. 3, each of which pieces has a silent beat just before its end; and in the Scherzo-

Impromptu, Op. 73, No. 2, and Scherzo, Op. 54, No. 5, both of which are punctuated by silent bars in several places throughout.

Lastly it may be noted that Grieg often used a plagal cadence, either plain or decorated, to end works of widely differing size and character, such as the second and third movements of the Concerto; the last movement of the Violin Sonata in G major; and *Gratitude*, Op. 62, No. 2, *Gade*, Op. 57, No. 2, *Folk-tune*, Op. 73, No. 4, and *The Students' Serenade*, Op. 73, No. 6.

Another point, Grieg's melodic construction, should be mentioned here, although it relates to his style in general rather than to his piano idiom in particular. Griegian melody is usually short-breathed and segmented : it rarely unfolds like the frond of a fern, in one long, gracious curve, but generally uncurls in a series of short, oft-repeated sections, as if it were a spray of oak-leaves. That the method has a charm and fascination of its own, who could deny upon hearing the long introductory piano solo of the second movement of the Violin Sonata in C minor? Throughout these forty-four bars in 2/4 time, not only is every phrase four bars in length (Ex. 34), but the little opening figure of three ascending notes recurs as many as eleven times in various keys. Nevertheless, the passage conveys not the slightest feeling of monotony but betokens true inspiration and a firm sense of direction.

Grieg's harmonic equipment and its inter-relationship with the Norwegian folk-idiom is a subject of great interest : so great, indeed, that it has been made the basis of a longish monograph by a Swiss writer, Kurt von Fischer. His *Griegs Harmonik und die nord-ländische Folklore*[1] is an exhaustive treatise wherein the author, while by no means neglecting the poetic aspect of the composer's works, concentrates principally upon an intensive and scientific analysis of Grieg's harmonic resource. To those whose business it is to investigate the minutiæ of harmonic progression, the book is completely enthralling. To others whose approach to the master is a more purely musical one, it may prove somewhat disconcerting to find Grieg's subtle combinations of sound burdened with ponderous nomenclature or reduced to mathematical formulæ; for was not Grieg a harmonist by instinct rather than by calculation? His own words, quoted by his Norwegian biographer, David Monrad-Johansen, are both reassuring and enlightening. 'The realm of harmony,' he said, ' was always my dream-world, and my harmonic sense was a mystery, even to myself. I have found that the sombre

[1] Berne and Leipzig, 1938.

depth of our folk-music has its foundation in its unsuspected harmonic possibilities. In my treatment of the folk-songs of Op. 66, and others, too, I have tried to give expression to my perception of their latent harmonies.'

It is in the systematic examination of these 'latent harmonies' and of Grieg's manner of revealing them, that Fischer's book is of particular interest. He points out that Grieg's harmony was never more typical than when he was most closely concerned with actual Norwegian folk-music, and it is significant that of the many music-type illustrations included in the book, the majority are quotations from the collections of folk-tune transcriptions, while a number of others are drawn from works of predominantly national character, such as the *Scenes from Folk Life*, Op. 19, and *Peer Gynt*. These compositions give an excellent idea of the particular fashion in which various folk-song characteristics influenced Grieg's craftsmanship and were responsible for the delightful blending of the primitive and the elegant which is one of the distinguishing attributes of his work. A few of the points which relate more specifically to the piano works may be briefly surveyed.

The indeterminate nature of tunes, such as *Lok og Bådnlåt*, and *Liten var Guten*, Op. 66, Nos. 6 and 9, which finish upon a note other than the tonic, caused Grieg to obscure the tonality of a piece by introducing chords foreign to the key, either before or at its close. The fluctuation of a tune between major and minor required from him an extensive use of chords of both the harmonic and melodic minor, as is shown in the *Bridal Song*, Op. 17, No. 6. Restricted melodic interest in a tune led him to great enterprise in the piling up of tonal devices for the purposes of contrast and colour —even when the harmonic scheme varied little, as may be seen in the Halling, Op. 17, No. 7, or, better still, in the *Gangar*, Op. 54, No. 2, where the cumulative effect is a powerful one. A series of rising or falling thirds in a melody, such as those in *Det er den störste Dårlighed* and *Siri Dale Visen*, Op. 66, Nos. 2 and 4, caused him to expand the triad into chords of the seventh and ninth. Instead of resolving these chords conventionally, the composer allowed them to melt into one another like the colours of the rainbow, momentarily dissolving the tonality and creating an atmosphere of vagueness. A short ostinato figure in a melody obliged him to employ all manner of harmonies in order to avoid monotony, as is well exemplified in *Morgo ska du få gifte deg*, Op. 66, No. 10. An even more telling illustration of his apparently inexhaustible power of diversifying a melody full of repetitions is to be found in the middle section of the first *Norwegian Dance* for piano duet, Op. 35, where, within the space of a couple of pages, a few bars of melody are harmonised not only over a tonic pedal, a submediant pedal and a dominant pedal successively and as an inner voice between an upper and lower submediant pedal too; but also in several other striking ways above independently moving basses. Small wonder that Grieg's sense of harmony was a mystery, even to himself!

6

The Songs

By

Astra Desmond

THE HUNDRED-AND-FORTY-ODD SONGS Grieg published fall conveniently into four main groups, according as they are settings of German, Danish, Norwegian Riksmål or Norwegian Landsmål poetry. It is, therefore, worth while to consider for a moment the main features of the poetry of each group. Grieg was very sensitive to the literary quality of poetry, and his music expresses very remarkably the characteristics of the poems he set. The two chief German poets that he used, Heine and Chamisso, are too well known to need discussion here, but a few words about the Scandinavian poets may be useful.

His first Scandinavian songs were settings of Danish poets, chiefly H. C. Andersen—known here as the author of the fairy-tales—and Chr. Richardt. Their poetry was chiefly notable for its lucidity and graceful, cultivated style, its descriptions of the milder aspects of nature and a gentle piety. Its chief defect was a tendency to redundance: Edmund Gosse remarks[1] that 'The innocence of all these amiable poets had no parallel elsewhere in Europe'. The notable exception was Holger Drachmann, who belonged to a younger generation and, to quote Edmund Gosse again, was 'like a cosmic force, ebullient and capricious. In him the poetic art of Denmark, hitherto so gentle in sound and moderate in radiance, seems to be elevated and summed up in the harmonious thunders of an earth-quake and the glare of a volcano'. It will be seen how Grieg's music reacted to the influence of this poetry—even to the redundance, though already there are signs of his tougher Norwegian fibre evident in songs like Op. 5, No. 4, *Min Tanke er et maegtigt Fjeld* (My thought is like a mighty mountain).

His first choice among his own countrymen fell upon Andreas Munch, but as this poet was one of the least characteristic of the Norwegians, he effected no change in Grieg's style. It was only

[1] *Oxford Book of Scandinavian Verse*, pp. 19–20.

when he turned to the great national poet Björnstjerne Björnson that the real Norwegian Grieg appeared. Björnson was the embodiment of all that was best in the Norwegian character—vital, spontaneous, robust, with a deep love of his native land and a superb gift for writing lovely lyrics, which he scattered about his prose writings. He was just what Grieg needed to stir all his enthusiasm and take him out of the easy-going ways of the preceding years.

The other great poet of that time was Henrik Ibsen, four years older than Björnson. Though not essentially a lyric poet, he gave Grieg material for three of his most famous songs. The extreme concentration and economy of Ibsen's verse set one of the most difficult problems to the translator, but they gave Grieg an exercise in developing that superb economy which is so remarkable a feature of such songs as Op. 25, Nos. 2, *En svane* (A Swan), and 5, *Borte* (Departed), and Op. 70, No. 3, *Lys Nat* (Lucent Night). A third poet upon whom he drew very largely was his friend John Paulsen. Paulsen was not in the same class as the two great poets just mentioned, but he provided lyrics for some very lovely songs, though it must be confessed he also provided the poems for some songs we could wish Grieg had left unwritten. Vilhelm Krag, the poet of Op. 60, No. 3, *Mens jeg venter* (While I wait), then only a young man, gave Grieg material for some fine songs in 1894.

The fourth group contains songs set to poetry by A. O. Vinje and Arne Garborg. Here it should be explained that in Norway there are two languages, one of which, the ordinary Riksmål, is, except for slight differences in spelling, etc., and a great difference in pronunciation, almost identical with Danish. In 1842, the year before Grieg was born, the great lexicographer Ivar Aasen began to make a comparative study of the various country dialects of Norway. Finally he devoted himself to creating a literary language based on dialect and Old Norse. The more violent nationalists took up this language with great ardour, and many writers adopted it. It is still taught in the schools in Norway, but though it has modified the Riksmål it has never displaced it. The two chief champions of Landsmål were Garborg and the peasant poet Vinje. The passionate nationalism of these two made an appeal to all that was most profound in Grieg, and some of his best songs were inspired by them. These are the songs which are least known outside Norway and which, if better known, would remove the charge sometimes made, that Grieg's songs are all ' pretty ' and ' lacking in depth '.

It would be interesting to know how Hugo Wolf's reputation

would have fared had he been fated to be judged entirely by badly translated versions of his songs. In a letter to Dr. Abraham, his publisher, dated January 27, 1892, Grieg wrote :

> I believe that even my best songs can never become ' popular ' in Germany. If the Nordic language were a cultural idiom, then perhaps —just as we always sing the masters of the German *Lied* in the original, even Schumann and Schubert, in spite of the many translations we have.

It is a tribute to the musical worth of his songs that in spite of this drawback and in spite of bad translations a handful of them have achieved world-wide popularity.

The problem of translation is a difficult one, especially when words and music are a close unity, as in the best of Grieg's songs. The similarities between German and Norwegian should make translating into the former language comparatively easy, but even if well done, there is the loss of colour and a heaviness which is almost worse than a complete change of sound. The Scandinavian consonants are light and ' clean '-sounding, e.g. ' Min svane, du stumme, du stille ' (with clear ' s ' sounds as in English) compared with ' Mein Schwan, du stummer, du stiller ', with the thick German ' sh ' sound. A critic once remarked that when sung in Norwegian, ' the whole atmosphere of the songs changed from the fustiness of later nineteenth-century German romanticism to the bright clean air of the fjords '.

There is also the difficulty of words like ' svane ' in Op. 25, No. 2, *En svane* : the last words of the song are like a sigh—' en svane '— but neither German nor English has a disyllabic word, and we get the dreadful ' Ein Schwan doch.' or, not much better, ' a swan thou '. There is, however, no excuse for the German translator's ' wonnigen ' in the fifth bar. The mere sight of that word is enough to send any singer (especially if the *pp* in the piano part has not been observed) into a paroxysm of sentiment, and coupled with a rising phrase to a luscious high F a crescendo is quite irresistible. But the poet says ' hverken slag eller trille ', literally ' neither throb nor trill ' (gave warning of a voice), so that the phrase should be pianissimo and almost expressionless. Indeed, in the manuscript the voice part is marked *pp* sempre tranquillo and in the full score of the orchestral version *pp* senza cresc.

Another bad example is in Op. 25, No. 3, *Stambogsrim* (Verse for an Album). The climax of the song is very dramatic. In the

73

eighth bar, having likened his love to a star which was 'joy's messenger that went', he has a semiquaver rest for the catch in the breath before the verb is repeated with the preposition that alters the whole sense—'went out' (i.e., became extinguished) (Ex. 62*a*); this the translator blandly ignores, removing the rest and giving 'du täuschtest mich' (Ex. 62*b*), thus destroying the whole point of the song. In most cases the English version seems to have been made from the German one; in this case it is doubtful if the author of the English version knew Norwegian, German or English.

Few, if indeed any, of the published translations were made by people who had any knowledge of Norwegian. Poor Grieg was constantly complaining about this in his letters, and in the Bergen Museum there is a manuscript of one of the songs of Op. 33 with German words written over the Norwegian ones in Grieg's own hand, evidently as a guide to the translator. Perhaps the crowning example of mistranslation is one published version of the lullaby from *Peer Gynt*. It is the exquisite song sung by Solveig over Peer when he returns at the end of his life, which she sings as the curtain descends. The translator unfortunately had not read the play, for this is how the refrain appears:

> Sleep my own little baby, sleep.
> I will watch as I rock the cradle
> Now is the time to say good-bye to play.

> Baby has played upon his mother's knee
> Till the close of day, sleepy is he,
> Now into dreamland has my baby gone.

Grieg's earliest songs appeared as Op. 10, settings of four Danish poems. They are of interest historically, but not otherwise. The first songs of any importance are Op. 2, *Four Songs for Alto*, to texts by Heine and Chamisso. These were written later than Op. 10, when he was a student at Leipzig, at the age of eighteen or nineteen. As is to be expected, they show a strong German influence, and two at least are very remarkable songs. He proved deeply susceptible to the inspiration of Heine's poetry. *Eingehüllt in graue Wolken* shows a remarkable feeling for the grim humour of the poem and a considerable gift for colour in the piano part. The strong rhythm of the piano introduction, however, reveals the northerner and gives a foretaste of the composer of *Efteraars-stormen* (The Autumn Storm) and *Tak for dit råd* (Thanks for thy rede). In *Ich stand in dunkeln Träumen* he has drawn his inspiration straight from Schubert, though his setting in no way resembles Schubert's own. This is a really beautiful song which deserves performance. Chamisso's *Die Müllerin* is also a good song. Op. 4, six more German songs, appears a year or so later. Of these, No. 2, *Morgenthau* (Morning dew) (Chamisso), and No. 3, *Abschied* (Farewell) (Heine), are wholly charming in a Schumannesque way; No. 5, *Das alte Lied* (The Ancient Song) (Heine), is interesting because of its archaic ballad style and economy of means, while the jolly No. 4, *Jägerlied* (Hunting song) (Uhland), forecasts *Der Jäger* (The Hunter) (Schulz) of a later date. No. 6, *Wo sind sie hin?* (Whither have they fled?) (Heine), shows considerable power and is remarkable for a long and expressive postlude; cf. Op. 39, No. 6, *Hörer jeg sangen klinge* (When I hear that song) (Rolfsen, after Heine).

For many years Grieg wrote no more German songs. When he did so again in 1889 he had found and developed his Norwegian personality, so that no one would think that the songs of Op. 48 were written by a German. It is interesting to note that in an interview with a London newspaper reporter at about this time Grieg, in answer to the question ' Has Norwegian nature still the same influence over and inspiration for you? ', replied, ' Personally speaking—yes; but in my music I am no longer so exclusively Norwegian as I was . . . my later works are not so pronouncedly representative of Scandinavian music. I have travelled about and become more European, more cosmopolitan.'

However this may be, even these settings of German texts have so definitely the mark of the Norwegian upon them that some people have been misled into thinking Grieg originally set the music to translations; but this is not the case. Oddly enough, the least interesting of these songs is the one by Heine, *Gruss*. No. 2, *Dereinst Gedanke mein* (Geibel), however, is very beautiful and moving. It is, as a rule, difficult for a Hugo Wolf lover to feel enthusiasm for anyone else's setting of a poem set by him, but these two settings are so different that it is possible to love them both. Wolf approaches this song as an intellectual, and we feel him trying to convince himself of the truth of the words and not quite succeeding until the end of the song. Grieg approaches it with resignation and a simple faith, religious in its feeling, that is very moving. No. 3, *Lauf der Welt* (Uhland), a gay light-hearted little song, is much enhanced if singers will resist the temptation to disobey Grieg's instruction to sing the last ' Ich liebe dich ' senza crescendo. No. 4, *Die verschwie-gene Nachtigall* (Walter von der Vogelweide), would be wholly enchanting were it not that in places the words are very awkwardly set to the music. No. 5, *Zur Rosenzeit* (Goethe), deserves to be sung more often. Its lovely melody over a rather Schumannesque accompaniment, gives place to a more passionate and very Griegish middle section, returning to the first subject at the end. The last song is the famous *Der Traum*, a song to delight the heart of any tenor with a good mezza voce. These songs are dedicated to Ellen Nordgren, the great Swedish Wagnerian soprano, who, as Ellen Gulbransen, sang some of Grieg's songs, notably *En Svane* and *Fra Monte Pincio* (From Mount Pincio) all over the world.

Another excellent song, *Der Jäger* (Schulz), appears among the posthumous works dated 1905, but it seems much more probable that it was written at the same time as Op. 48, as was also possibly the little *Osterlied*, also without opus number. In 1905 Grieg was such a very sick man and was writing little, if any music, that it is difficult to believe that such an extremely vigorous and jolly song as *Der Jäger* could have been written then.

Grieg left Leipzig in 1862, and after a year at home in Norway, he went to Copenhagen, then a centre of Scandinavian culture. Danish musicians were very much under the influence of the German school, that of Mendelssohn in particular, and so Grieg was still to be surrounded by that very influence which is the bane of all Scandi-navian composers who are not strong enough to rise free of it, once they have absorbed from it all that is of value to them.

Leaving aside the first Scandinavian songs, Op. 10 referred to above, Grieg's first volume of Danish songs is Op. 5. It is dedicated to the author of all its lyrics, H. C. Andersen. Here we have the sparkling little *To brune Öjne* (Two Brown Eyes), written upon getting engaged to Nina Hagerup, a fine musician and interpreter, though she had not a great voice. It is probably due to the fact that the composer had at his side so fine a singer that his songs are all so ' singable '. There are still people who remember her incomparable singing of songs like *Med en primula veris* (With a Primrose), *Med en vandlilje* (With a Water-lily), etc., while Grieg himself always said of her that she was the one true interpreter of his songs. The most famous of all his songs is in this opus : *Jeg elsker Dig* (I love thee). Possibly owing to the fact that the German ' translator ' chose to add a second verse, singers frequently sing this song through twice. The manuscript at Bergen makes it clear that neither a repeat nor a second verse was intended by the composer, and the song is infinitely more effective and convincing thus. It is the outpouring of a very young man very much in love, and a little awed by the wonder of first love. On the second beat of the first reiterated 'jeg elsker Dig' both the manuscript and the Scandinavian edition have an accelerando marked, so that the emotion rises to the climax of the last 'jeg elsker Dig', both by acceleration of tempo and a big crescendo. To go back to the beginning and do the whole thing again seems to be an anticlimax, robbing the song of all its spontaneity and sincerity. The other two songs, *Digterhjertet* (The Poet's Heart) and *Min Tanke er et maegtigt Fjeld* (My thought is a great mountain) are both good, especially the latter, a magnificent song for a baritone. Curiously enough these are almost all short songs; not yet has the Danish spirit quite captured him.

He wrote a number of songs of varying quality during this and the following few years. In Op. 9, settings of Andreas Munch, we have a fine ballad *Harpen* (The Harp) and an unusual *Vuggesang* (Lullaby), written for a man's voice to lull his motherless babe, which has a lovely melody, but rather too many verses for public performance without a cut. These are actually the first Norwegian texts he used, but as the poems are not particularly Norwegian in spirit they did not deflect him from what we may call his Danish style. Op. 15, No. 2, *Kjaerlighed* (Love), by H. C. Andersen, is another lovely Schumannesque song, but for modern taste the three verses are rather too many and it is more satisfactory to omit the second. One of the best songs of the period is *Efteraarsstormen* (The Autumn Storm), Op. 18, No. 4, basis of the *Autumn* overture. The poem by Richardt is a delightful one, with charming touches, such as the idea of the blast of the storm-wind causing the forest to lose its green hat, the picture of the poor people blessing the storm because it gives them firewood to keep them warm, and the thought of the kindly snow healing the wounds of earth and covering them until the spring calls the seeds to grow. There is a delightful piano part, and in its changing moods the song is full of colour and variety. It is interesting to compare Grieg's treatment of the snows of winter in this song with the same subject fifteen years later in *Våren* (Spring), Op. 33, No. 2. The objective approach here is very different from the deep subjective emotion of the later song. *Udfarten* (The Departure), another Munch setting, is a narrative song, through-composed and with some beautiful passages, but suffering from the defects of the over-long lyric.

77

There remain a few more Danish songs (Op. 18, to texts by H. C. Andersen) composed after he left Copenhagen : a charmingly fresh little honeymoon song for a light voice, *Vandring i Skoven* (Wandering in the Woods) with its delightful staccato passage in the second and third bars of the animato section, *Poesien* (Poetry), a fine, sweeping melody over a harp-like accompaniment—the weakness of this song being its strophic form, each verse having a climax that sounds as if it should be the end of the song—the enchanting *Hytten* (The Hut), with its yodel-like voice-part, and the naïve little *Rosenknoppen* (Rosebuds).

Grieg wrote no more Danish songs until many years later, in 1886, when the famous Danish poet Holger Drachmann came to Norway, and the two set off on a walking tour over Jotunheim, with the purpose of collaborating in a set of songs which appeared under the title *Fra Fjeld og Fjord* (From Mountain and Fjord). The result is frankly disappointing. From the songs it seems as if the only impression this tour among some of the grandest scenery in Norway left upon the susceptible poet was the memory of various girls they met in the course of it. With the exception of the Prologue and Epilogue, the cycle deals with the charms of these young women. The poems had little inspiration for Grieg, and with the exception of *Ragnhild*, which is delightfully gay and fresh, the cycle is not in his best vein. One cannot help regretting that Drachmann did not wait until after the tour was over and the charmers forgotten before writing his memories.

Far more successful are the settings of the same poet's words three years later. Op. 49 contains two of Grieg's very best songs, *Vug, o Vove* (Rock, O Wave) and *Forårsregn* (Spring Rain). The former suffers from being too long, but if verse two—musically identical with verse one—is omitted, the song gains far more in unity than the poem loses. Drachmann's exuberance is finely matched by the music. Grieg is always very successful in reproducing the effect of water, and the rocking accompaniment to the easy, swinging voice part gives a delightful impression of the boat swaying on the water. Here may be quoted one of the gems of the ' translator's ' art :

> Waft, O waters, with wavelets bland
> Lightly our vessel gliding,
> Stroke us stream, with thy cooling hand
> Over our quarter sliding.

There follows a quasi-recitative section over the ever-changing harmonies so dear to Grieg, and the song ends with a magnificent climax.

Forårsregn is a setting of a delightful poem, quite free from the over-exuberance to which Drachmann is sometimes prone. It is a picture of the spring rain falling through the leaves upon the gravel, making a faint music as if fairy fingers were playing upon tiny instruments. Memories of lost youth are revived, but as the rain brings refreshment to tired earth, so such tears ease the heavy heart. The piano has a charming descending figure, expressive of the soft rain-drops falling, and the voice part is full of colour and expression. In these songs the Danish influence is modified partly by Grieg's greater skill and experience and also by the fact that Drachmann, though still given to a certain prolixity, was a much more vital personality than his predecessors. *Julesne* (Christmas Snow) has some lovely passages, but is much too long for modern taste. *Saa du Knösen* (Did you see the lad?) is a boisterous man's song, marred by having too many verses in strophic form. *Nu er Aftnen lys og lang* (Now the evening's light and long) is attractive but needs to be sung in Danish, a language not to be recommended to any but a native.

The last Danish songs to be set by Grieg were also the last he ever wrote, and it is interesting to see how he gets lured again into the diffuseness of his earlier period. In 1900 he wrote two volumes of songs to the poems of Otto Benzon. Two songs only are up to his best standard; one of them is outstanding. The first, *Der gynger en Båd* (A boat is rocking), is a fine song, with a delicious watery gurgle in the piano introduction; it is full of colour and exuberant freshness, remarkable when one considers that most of the preceding winter had been spent by the composer in a sanatorium, battling against the disease which was to cost him his life in a few years' time. He was very fond of *Ved Moders Grav* (At Mother's Grave), a fine dirge-like song which, he said, ' should sound like an Amati violin, or rather violoncello '; but the poem is unattractive to English ears, which are loath to hear too much about dead mothers. *Drömme* (Dream) has some lovely things in it, but lacks unity. *Eros*, Op. 70, No. 1, is a favourite with singers, being effective vocally, but it is not true Grieg, and, to one person at least, its pseudo-Wagnerism sounds rather pretentious. The same criticism applies to *Digtervise* (Poet's Song), though this was a great favourite of the composer and was written for his friend the famous baritone, Thorwald Lammers. The gem of the whole collection is *Lys Nat*. Here is the true Grieg, no swelling of the chest and tiptoeing to look like the burly Drachmann, but the fine sensitive artist making a handful of notes convey the paleness of the northern summer night, when the sun sets only to rise again almost at once, and the lover bewails the shortness of the night. In this song it is the nights of Norway, not of Denmark, that are in the composer's mind, and instinctively he turns to his more concentrated Norwegian style of writing.

In the posthumous works there is a lovely little lullaby, *Julens Vuggesang* (Christmas Lullaby) by Langsted, dated 1900, the same year as the Benzon songs. It has four short verses and is one of those moving little songs Grieg could write so effectively: a simple and lovely tune over a beautifully harmonised rocking accompaniment.

The story of Grieg's meeting with the fiery red-headed patriot Rikard Nordraak in Copenhagen in 1864 is well known. The composer of the National Song of Norway, *Ja vi elsker dette landet,* had a powerful influence upon him and encouraged him to study his native literature and folk music. Grieg, writing of their first meeting, in a letter to a friend says :

> Nordraak held out his hand and said 'We two great men will assuredly get on together'. Up to that moment I had never thought of the possibility of being or becoming a great man. I was a pupil, nothing more; till then, timid, shy and sickly, but that confidence of victory was just medicine for me.

Under the influence of Nordraak, whose untimely and tragic death deprived Norway of a great musical genius, Grieg was persuaded to look for inspiration in his own native country. In his first important Norwegian songs he went to the most Norwegian poet of all—Björnson. These songs are settings of four lyrics which appear in the prose romance, *The Fishermaiden*. At once we see a change in Grieg's style. There is an economy and strength in Norwegian poetry not to be found in Danish, and as Grieg breaks away from foreign influences and begins to find his Norwegian soul, we find a new economy in his music, which, used with the mastery of technique gained from his previous teachers, gives us song-writing of a high order.

There is no trace of sentimentality in his picturesque setting of the lovely *Det förste möde* (The first meeting). This song occurs in Björnson's novel after an exquisite passage describing the two young lovers' meeting and their sudden realisation of each other's love, as they sit among the trees by the fjord in the evening sunshine, the only sounds their own hearts beating and a horn sounding in the distance. Grieg caught their hushed wonder in the dreamy opening—the Scandinavian edition marks the song 'Langsomt og drömmende' (slow and dreamily)—and then with ever-extending phrases expresses their rapture, ending with a superb sweep from top A flat to low C (Ex. 63a). Here the German translator set his words very badly to music (Ex. 63b); the hurried ' sehnsuchts . . . ', followed by the excessive stress on '. . . vollem' spoils the original phrase with its comma break and repetition of ' et under '.

Jeg giver mit digt til våren (I give my song to the Spring), and *God morgen* (Good Morning) are charming songs for a light soprano. It is said that Nina Grieg did not sing all the trills marked in *God morgen*, but that is a matter for individual taste. In *Jeg giver mit digt* note the lovely return to the key of B, after the mock-angry changes of key rising to the climax in the twenty-ninth bar. The last of the Fishermaiden's songs, *Tak for dit råd*, is one of the finest songs Grieg ever wrote. The strength of its rhythm has been much weakened by the translations which add a note before the opening phrase. The verse should begin with a dactyl and the rhythm should be preserved rigidly on the long notes, the accompanist being restrained from his kindly impulses to save the singer's breath by hurrying the arpeggio and silent bars.

A visit to Rome inspired the lovely *Fra Monte Pincio*. It is strange to read this poem now. Björnson looking down over Rome had visions of the day when

> She will rise again, Rome will awaken,
> Blaze forth one night, rousing Italy's glory.
> Bells will be ringing, and cannon will roar
> Mem'ries of glory the future enflame.

What would he have thought had he known just how uselessly his prophecy was to be fulfilled? Quite different in colour is this song from either the Danish or Norwegian songs. A warmth suffuses it, and the melody's rise and fall would delight an Italian's heart. This is one of the songs Grieg orchestrated, thereby enhancing it considerably.

Prinsessen (The Princess) is in ballad style, written with that moving simplicity which Grieg could achieve so successfully. Under the title *Twilight Fancies* this is one of the many Scandinavian poems Delius later used for his own songs. There are various unimportant settings of Björnson's poems, but the only others which call for remark are *Dulgt kjaerlighed* (Hidden Love), another poem

F

also set by Delius, slightly reminiscent of Solveig's song, and in which the restlessness and discontent of the disappointed lover is well shown in the rather jerky phrases, which change beautifully into the tranquillo of the last verse; and a beautiful song that is all we have of the oratorio *Fred* (Peace), which was to have been written during the eighteen-nineties in collaboration with Björnson, but never materialised.

Of the ten songs to Ibsen's poetry, at least three are famous. Solveig's song is in every soprano's repertory, and is one of the songs that only a soprano should attempt. This is, incidentally, the only one of Grieg's songs modelled on a folk-tune.[1] A Paris critic, Pierre Lalo, the composer's son, once informed his readers that all Grieg's songs were stolen from folk-tunes. Grieg was much hurt by this and wrote indignantly to Frants Beyer (April 1903): '*You* know that out of all my hundred-odd songs, only one, Solveig's song, has borrowed a tune—no more.' This idea has had a very persistent life, and there are still people to-day who blandly repeat the fable. Perhaps it is a tribute to the national character of his music.

Less well known is the exquisite *Solveigs vuggesang* (Lullaby). This needs the orchestra to realise its full beauty. All the deep tenderness of the wife-mother is expressed here, and with sure dramatic instinct the final lines are marked forte, to be sung with increasing breadth and feeling as the sun—symbol of Solveig's faith—breaks upon the scene and the curtain gradually falls.

In the Scandinavian edition there are six songs in Op. 25, but No. 6, *En fuglevise* (A Bird-Song)—also set by Delius—is not a great loss : the poem is not as good as the others and the music, although it has charm, is not remarkable. No. 1 is the very Norwegian, dramatic *Spillemaend* (Fiddlers). It begins with the phrase, very characteristic of Grieg, which was used later in the G minor String Quartet (cf. Ex. 45, though in the song the melody has an initial up-beat and is in the major). The poem deals with the legend of one of the spirits that are supposed to dwell in every waterfall in Norway, who tries to lure the minstrel into his power, by promising him help to win his love. Over a tremolo accompaniment the struggle with the evil spirit is finely worked up to the climax, when too late the minstrel breaks free, to find his love already his brother's bride.

No. 2 is the famous and lovely *En svane*. The poem is in Ibsen's most concentrated style. It is quite reasonable to take the words literally as referring to a white swan, lying dead, after uttering its

[1] Cf. Ex. 82 and footnote on p. 108.

traditional swan-song, but Grieg certainly read more into the poem, as is shown by a letter he wrote to Finck about a Belgian singer, Grimand, saying : ' He sang wonderfully, with strong dramatic feeling. No Norwegian has the courage to give such a poem the musical expression worthy of such a tragic subject '. To the Northern mind the swan is always associated with the idea of the soul (cf. Op. 59, No. 5, *Farvel*). There is a story that, at about the time this poem was written, Ibsen had had a hopeless passion for a young girl. She had seemed cold and unresponsive, so that, discouraged, he found consolation elsewhere, only to discover too late that she had loved him all the time, but had been too shy to reveal the fact. This story certainly gives a likely clue to the inner meaning of the poem, though, of course, it may be quite untrue. Thus the swan could be the soul of the girl, anxiously concealing the sleeping elf—that is, her hidden feelings—until too late, in death, her confession came : ' You sang dying, you were indeed a swan—a swan! ' There are a number of omissions in the expression marks of the German edition, most of which occur, however, in the orchestral score. The *pp* sempre tranquillo in bar 5 has already been referred to; in bar 21 the crescendo should continue to the very end of the bar, instead of diminuendo as in the piano copy. In bar 26 *p* should be meno *p* in both piano and voice, and in the fourth bar from the end, after the pianissimo high F, there should be a crescendo on the word ' svane ' ('Schwan ' or ' swan ') up to *mf*, the piano echoing the phrase warmly. The lento bar should be pianissimo, and the last ' en svane ' just a sigh. The composer's direction, ' Langsomt og tilbageholdt ', is not rightly conveyed by ' Andante ben tenuto '; it means slowly and held back, ' tilbageholdt ' being the adjective used for ' bated ' breath. There should be this feeling of passion held back, which breaks out in the agitato section. Grieg liked the arpeggiando chords in the last six bars very much spread.

Stambogsrim is another beautiful song; its fate at the translator's hands has already been discussed. No. 4, *Med en vandlilje* (With a Water-lily) is well known and one of the most charming of songs— one of those that Nina sang so enchantingly. It is an example of the extreme care with which Grieg marked his wishes, and of the sad fact that those marks are so often completely disregarded by performers. To begin with the song is marked ' Hurtig med skjaelmeri ': fast, and with—the word means ' roguery ', but that conjures up visions of archness, so perhaps one might say with ' playfulness '. The innumerable changes of tempo give the song the impetuous restlessness of youth hovering on the brink of passion; the accompaniment races off whenever it is left alone, to be brought back by the voice, as if the piano were the boy's thoughts racing ahead of the spoken word. The song gains enormously if singers will observe where the $<$ $>$ comes (Ex. 64), instead of making the usual crescendo on 'bringer'. It is interesting to note that the staccato marks in verses 3 and 4 in the German edition do not occur in the Norwegian edition, and one is tempted to think that Grieg found the German too heavy and smooth compared with the original words, which being very consonantal make a staccato effect naturally.

No. 5, *Borte*, is one of Grieg's masterpieces—the short matching phrases corresponding exactly to the rhyming verses, a sparse accompaniment consisting mostly of octaves with the third—a single page of music, but a whole picture is in it, and a whole tragedy. For once the German translation is good. Henzen was a poet with some musical knowledge, and though he fails often he has some good work to his credit, notably this song, and the delightful Op. 26, No. 2, *Jeg reiste en dejlig sommerkvaeld* (I wandered one lovely summer eve). The little *Margretes vuggevise* (Margaret's Lullaby) was written long before, in 1868, just after Grieg's daughter was born. Alas, little Alexandra was fated to climb the angel's ladder for ever, only thirteen months later.

We turn from the two giants of Norway to lesser men. However, lesser men can often write very good lyrics, and John Paulsen has given us *Med en primula veris*, one of the most loved of Grieg's songs. This fresh and lovely thing is too well known to need description, but it may be well to remark in passing that in the Scandinavian edition there is a repeat from the pause bar back to the beginning. No. 1, *Et håb* (A Hope), is fairly well known, a jubilant song with a fine tune and a quite enchanting piano postlude. No. 2, *Jeg reiste en dejlig sommerkvaeld*, referred to above, is a dainty song in folk-song style, very grateful for a light voice. No. 3, *Den aergjerrige* (Ambition), appears only in the Scandinavian edition, which is a pity, as it is a fine song with an interesting piano part and a good climax. No. 5, *På skogstien* (On the Woodland Path) is rather lovely with its melancholy chromatic treatment. It is very representative of Grieg in a nostalgic Norwegian mood. The other Paulsen songs were written some eighteen years later. Of Op. 58, if we except No. 2, the less said the better. We are told that Homer sometimes nods, but we can almost hear Grieg's snores in some of these songs. No. 2, *Til Norge* (To Norway), however, is a beautiful, sincere poem addressing Norway as the mother who has nourished her children and to whom the poet renders loving homage.

Op. 59 is a set of elegiac poems, all of which are attractive, but the best is *Til En—I* (To One), another of those songs which show how much Grieg could achieve with slight means. The contrast between the young girl as the Spring, and the ageing man as Autumn, is simply and beautifully done, by using the same phrase in C major for the young girl and in C minor for the man. A poignant passage of falling chords illustrates the falling of the leaves of lost illusion as the final renunciation is made. *Til En—II* is also good, with slight reminiscences of *Tristan*. No. 5, *Farvel* (Farewell), gives us a picture of the swan flying to the south, the swan the symbol of the soul of the dead. This is a most heartfelt and moving song.

Of the other poets used by Grieg the most important is Vilhelm Krag, five of whose poems he set at this same period, 1894, and published as Op. 60. Best known is the charmingly sunny and carefree *Mens jeg venter*, No. 3, with its descriptive piano part and its delightful little descending chromatic passages for the voice. No. 1 is worthy of attention, a charming poem about Little Kirsten spinning her bridal linen and dreaming over her ring of gold while the cuckoo calls outside. The piano discreetly suggests the spinning-wheel and the note of the cuckoo. No. 4, *Der skreg en fugl* (There screamed a bird), is a remarkable song. It is introduced and ended with a figure on the piano which is a striking imitation of a seagull's cry. After Grieg's death this theme was found in one of his little notebooks, and written under it was ' Gull's cry heard in Hardanger fjord'. The song gives a wonderful impression of the cold desolate waters and a solitary bird with flapping broken wing, floating out to sea. The last, *Og jeg vil ha mig en hjertenskjær* (I will have a sweetheart), is a vigorous song, full of high spirits, with a tune that might almost have been a folk-tune. The accompaniment is very ingenious and very brilliant. Is it ungenerous to criticise it as being just a little too brilliant? Three other songs deserve mention. Op. 39, No. 5, *Ved en ung hustrus båre* (At the bier of a young wife) is a touching poem and very beautifully set, but one cannot help wishing that there had been only one verse. *Odalisken synger* (The Odalisque's Song) (Bruun), without opus number, is an excursion into the exotic. One wonders whether Delius knew this song when he wrote his *In the Seraglio Garden*.

Before considering the last group of songs mention must be made of the *Barnlige Sanger* (Children's Songs), Op. 61, which are quite delightful and have been given an attractive English version by Lady Macfarren. These are real children's songs, rhythmic, tuneful and simple and yet always interesting musically. No. 1, *Havet* (Sea Song) (Rolfsen), a most spirited little song in the Lydian mode, was a special favourite of the composer. Nos. 3 and 5, *Lok* (Cow Call) (Björnson) and *Kveldsang for Blakken* (Dobbin's good-night) (Rolfsen), are set with a delicate gaiety and humour that is enchanting. No. 7 *Faedrelands-Salme* (Fatherland's Psalm), is a noble setting of Rolfsen's version of Runeberg's famous poem.

Whenever Grieg was most unhappy he was drawn to the poets who sang in Landsmål, and so as early as 1868 we find him setting the touching poem *Millom Rosor* (Among the Roses) by Kristofer Janson, just after his only child had died. The song tells of a mother laughing and happy with her child among the roses, then in the second verse the mother mourns her child, now dead among the roses. Poem and music both ring true. With unerring instinct Grieg set it in simple folk-song style.

In 1877, after the production of *Peer Gynt*, Grieg felt the need for rest and spiritual refreshment so he retired to Lofthus, on the Hardanger fjord, a favourite resort of his and one of the loveliest spots in all Norway. Here he came across Landstad's *Ancient Norwegian Folklore*. One of these old Norse poems, *Den Bjergtegne* (The Mountain Thrall), made a profound impression upon him. He was on the verge of a period of sterility and frustration and this tale of the man, lost in the mountains, lured on by the elusive Erl-King's daughter, seemed to express his own mood. His first intention was to write a large-scale work with chorus, but as he could not find suitable texts, he contented himself with the one poem, and set it for baritone solo with string orchestra and two horns, and it appeared as Op. 32, *Den Bergtekne*. As was his wont when setting folklore or folk-style poetry, he set the poem very simply in ballad style. The horns give out an expressive theme which is taken up by the violins first and later by the voice, over a mournful descending bass on the lower strings. At the appearance of the Erl-King's daughter the movement quickens and the man's bewilderment is emphasised by the disjointed and reiterated chords in the strings over a tremolando bass, leading to an agitato section as the enchantress leads him ever further from his path. In his despair, the first theme recurs for a moment; then, with a complete change of mood, he sadly watches the fishes and animals who all have mates while only he is lonely. After this rather sentimental and not very inspiring interlude the work ends with a repetition of the opening verse. The song is in Old Norse, but a modern version is printed under the original text. Grieg was deeply attached to this work and said that 'it was written with devotion . . . one of the best deeds of my life '.

It was after the period of strain referred to above that he suddenly found relief in the poems of the peasant poet A. O. Vinje. Two of these he had worked on previously, *Gamle Mor* (Old Mother) in 1873 and *Langs ei Aa* (Along the River) in 1877, but most of Op. 33 was written in one spate of composition. There was something in this language of the soil which appealed to all that was deepest in Grieg's nature, and drew from him some of his most intimate and deeply-felt music. A German critic, referring to the Vinje songs, once criticised him for his frequent use of the strophic form; had he been able to read the original poems he would have realised that Grieg's choice of this form was deliberate. The poetry is of the soil and the people of the soil, and he was unquestionably right in giving the songs the form of folk-songs, a form to which the construction of the poems lent itself perfectly; where it did not, as in the case of Nos. 5 and 6, he composed the songs through.

The first song, *Guten* (The Youth), with its strong rugged opening leading up to a great sweeping phrase at the end of each verse, was just the thing to suit his discouraged mood. The boy suffers and loses his love, but in the last verse he stands upon the ruins of his world and from that height at last can see far into the distance. Grieg for the last few years had fancied himself written out, and had spent the time in perfecting his technique, writing nothing; then, suddenly, it is as if this poem taught him the meaning of those sterile years, and his music gushes forth fresh and strengthened by his experience.

Våren (Spring) and *Den Sårede* (The Wounded Heart) are well known from their orchestral transcriptions, which possibly make them sound a little thin when performed in their original form with the piano. *Våren* is too long to be sung in its entirety to English audiences, though Norwegians can listen to the whole song, because both words and music are so lovely. The poignant melody of *Den Sårede* is well known. In *Tyttebaeret* (The Whortleberry) Grieg seems to have been a little overloaded by the slightly forced patriotism of the poem. *Langs ei aa* is not strophic in form. The picture of the tree bending down to kiss the stream that is slowly wearing away the soil from its roots, while the piano's persistent three-quaver figure suggests the movement of the water, and the comparison with youth's trust betrayed by false friends make a poignant song.

Eit Syn (A Vision), also composed through, with its dainty dance rhythm, gives a charming impression of a peasant lad too shy to approach his loved one. *Gamle Mor* is again in the folk-song style, a lovely tune, very skilfully harmonised, one of the few songs ever written in praise of a mother that is quite free from sentimentality, hard though it may be to believe from the English version. It was written as a tribute to Grieg's own mother, and has become nearly as dear to the Norwegians as one of their own folk-songs. *Det Förste* (The First) is not very interesting, but the next, *Ved Rundarne* (Return to Rundarne), describes the wanderer's emotion on returning to his native place in a lovely flowing melody that seems to remind us of Grieg's Scottish ancestry. Translated into Scots it could almost pass as a Scots song. *Et Vennestykke* (A Broken Friendship) is an exception in that the poem is written in Riksmål. It is very striking and full of bitterness. The one drawback is that the words, even in Norway, are apt to raise a smile, where a smile should not be. The published English version does not help with its

> False are friends, all,
> This offends all,
> Yet full well 'tis known
> One I deemed was mine, dear,
>   (O beware of thine, dear)
> Hence did wrest one;
> 'Twas the best one,
> From my side has flown!

The bitterness is well suggested by the discordant G sharp against the A natural of the dirge-like D minor chords.

Trudom (Faith) is a bitterly ironic poem set to an incongruous hymnlike tune. *Fyremål* (The Goal) is really quite unsuitable for foreigners to sing, as it is a glorification of Landsmål, and an admonition to good Norwegians to talk it always. This is a pity, for it is a fine dramatic song. It was later worked up as a piece for string orchestra and appeared with an orchestral version of Op. 21, No. 1, *Det Förste Möde*, as Op. 53, Nos. 1 and 2.

Another great champion of Landsmål was Arne Garborg. Some time in 1894–5 he published a volume of poems entitled *Haugtussa*. Not since the Vinje poems fifteen years before had anything made such an instantaneous appeal to Grieg's heart and imagination. He read the book voraciously and even conceived the idea of using it for a work on a major scale. He set several of the poems, but only eight were published, and they appeared as the *Haugtussa Sang-Cyclus* (Op. 67).

This poetry is intensely Norwegian in quite a different way from Vinje's. There is a tragic quality in Vinje which we do not find in *Haugtussa*. Vinje is preoccupied with human emotions and their relation to nature. His descriptions are generally bound up with some human experience. In *Våren* the ecstasy of a northern spring, so beautifully described, merely points the contrast with the sick man who will not live to see another spring. The little *Tyttebaeret* is not just a charming thing in itself, it is a peg on which to hang a patriotic song. Garborg, on the other hand, simply takes us by the hand into the valleys and up on to the mountain-sides, showing us the streams and flowers and the sweet wholesome life of the simple peasant folk for their own sake.

Having despaired in England at the difficulty of putting into English the *Haugtussa-Cyclus* poems, I repaired to a small mountain resort above Bergen with the only—very inadequate—dictionary available. The first day's walk revealed the very counterpart of Haugtussa's bilberry slopes, her saeter-hut with the kidlings staggering about, and the stream to which she brought her sorrows, so that several problems of translation were solved. The loveliness and the awe-inspiring scenery make a belief in magic a very strong characteristic of the peasants, and the little heroine of the book, Veslemöy (little maiden) earned the nickname of ' Haugtussa ' (Troll-maiden) because of her gift for seeing and hearing the troll- and fairy-folk. She has the misfortune to attract the desire of a troll, and the first song, *Det syng* (The Singing), is the song with which he tries to lure her to his mountain home. Grieg reverts quite deliberately and for a definite effect to the strophic style in all except two of the eight songs of the cycle. In *Det syng* the troll's evil nature is indicated by the rather brutal opening; then, finding the girl is not to be won by intimidation, he softens his tones to a seductive lilt in the second half of the verse. Terrified, the girl runs into her grandmother's room, and the second song, *Veslemöy*, gives us a most touching portrait. No epic heroine, this, but a pale, frightened girl, with slender form and grey visionary eyes. Tenderly we are told that her brow was fair, but low. Grieg's music perfectly matches the exquisite poem, and Veslemöy stands out clearly as a living person. In gayest spirits she takes her cow and sheep and goats out to graze, and in No. 3, *Blåbaerli* (Bilberry slopes) (see Ex. 93), we have a picture which anyone who has been to Norway will have seen a dozen times.

Hillsides covered with bilberries and animals grazing. The words are amusing and quaint in a way which cannot be reproduced in another language. A German biographer, recognising the difficulty, recommends singers either to sing it in the original or in English. He considers the German version sounds 'zu vulgär', in Norwegian it would sound 'urwüchsig', but in English it would be 'beinahe so amüsant wie ein Niggersong'!

In the fourth song, *Möte* (Meeting), Haugtussa awaits and finally meets her lover. With great tenderness poet and composer give us the shy, awkward meeting of the young inexperienced lovers, and the gradual breaking down of the barriers as evening draws them closer together. No. 5, *Elsk* (Love), is the first song to be composed right through. It begins with a sort of improvisation as the girl sings to herself that she is captured like a bird in the cage of love; thoughts and wishes pass through her mind in quick succession, and the music follows her thoughts through various tempi and various keys. In this song Grieg uses a device with the pedal, leaving it on right through the forty-second and subsequent bars, through the rests and the following octave passage, thereby giving the octaves a delightful bell-like sound. He uses this device again in Op. 60, No. 4, *Der skreg en fugl.*

No. 6, *Killingdans* (Kidlings' Dance), is an interlude of sheer fun. A shower of onomatopœic words and amusing alliterations and rhymes describes the antics of the baby goats on the hillside. Grieg has a most amusing figure in the piano, jaunty little semiquavers changing suddenly into stumbling little triplets. This song used to be a great favourite with Lilli Lehmann, we are told. In No. 7, *Vond Dag* (Evil Day), tragedy has overtaken Haugtussa. Her lover promised to come to her, even though it hailed, and he has failed her. In the book we are told that someone came to tell her he had been seen with a new love. The long sweeping phrases through a compass of an octave and a third are very beautiful and pathetic.

The last song, *Ved Gjaetle-Bekken* (By the Brook) is also composed right through. Here is nature-music of a high order, with a lovely piano part descriptive of the little brook, giving a vivid picture of any one of the thousands of little streams that ripple down a Norwegian mountain-side, now scarcely moving among the stones in the sunshine, now hidden in the thick moss, emerging again in a swirl to go rushing down the slope. Here Haugtussa brings her aching heart, and the brook wakens burning memories, then soothes her till, weary with weeping, she sinks down and lets its murmuring music lull her to sleep.

Grieg considered these his best songs. Certain it is that all his passionate love for Norway went into this music. Like the Vinje songs, they can never be popular outside Norway, and even so the cycle should be heard as a whole if its true beauty and worth are to be appreciated. Landsmål has longer vowel sounds than Riksmål, which makes it more beautiful to listen to. Grieg disliked the idea of *Haugtussa* being sung in Riksmål; how much more he would have disliked a German or English translation!

Not every one of Grieg's songs has been discussed here, nor has mention been made of the innumerable beautiful arrangements he made of folk and popular Norwegian songs. But it is hoped that enough has been said to convince the reader that instead of the half-dozen or so that are regularly heard, there are at least fifty or sixty that deserve serious attention in an estimate of Grieg's position as a song-writer.

His most serious fault is his frequent use of the strophic form. This is not a fault in itself, for even Schubert used this form frequently, and in some of his most famous songs, but it becomes a fault when each verse is finished off with a climax and a great flourish in the piano part, as in Op. 18, II, No. 1, *Poesien*. One should, however, remember that this was quite a regular custom among Grieg's predecessors and contemporaries. The strophic style in its most primitive form was extensively used by Norwegian and Danish composers, the only thing that differentiated many of the songs from the folk-songs being their inferiority. It is interesting to observe, however, that Grieg rarely used this form in either his German or Norwegian songs—except of course in the case of the Vinje and Garborg songs, where it was used for a definite reason—but only, to a great extent, in the Danish songs.

Occasionally his favourite device of working up a passage by a chromatic change of key, so successful in Op. 48, No. 5, *Zur Rosenzeit* becomes tiresome, as in Op. 70, No. 1, *Eros,* but generally his taste is faultless, and whenever he has a really fine poem he never fails us. He gives us no profound philosophy, but he gives with deep sincerity human joys and sorrows, and the beauty of nature, spontaneously and in language that goes straight to the heart. In his simplest songs, with rare exceptions, he is never banal. Always there is musical interest in the writing. Words and music are beautifully interwoven, the songs are a joy to both singer and pianist to study and perform, and—supreme test—the student does not easily tire of them.

Grieg's claim to greatness lies in the fact that he had the strength of personality to escape from the stranglehold of Teutonism and make the technique learned from Germany his instrument, not his master. Just as the Norwegian language translated into German becomes overloaded with the thicker gutteral sounds, so the Norwegian spirit loses its freshness and vitality when immersed in a turgid sea of Teutonism. Grieg's achievement was to give to the world the spirit of Norway in an international musical language. His best songs have failed to become popular, not so much because they are written in Norwegian as because so few singers have troubled to sing them; but they should be sung, for they add their distinctive colour and fragrance to the garland of song.

7

Works for the Stage

By

John Horton

NORWAY'S NATIONAL STAGE OWED its origin almost as much to musicians as to dramatists. When, in 1825, Waldemar Thrane set the lyrics in H. A. Bjerregaard's *Fjeldeventyret* (The Mountain Story), the earliest dramatic work to have a distinctively Norwegian theme, he was not only carrying on the common Scandinavian tradition of ballad-opera but also making an important contribution to the nationalist cause. Twenty-three years later Ole Bull returned from his concert tours in Europe and America to work out plans for a national academy of the arts. His object was to foster ' Norwegian drama, Norwegian actors, Norwegian music, and a Norwegian ballet '. In 1850 the first Norse theatre was inaugurated at Bergen. Among the first season's productions were Wergeland's ballad-opera *Fjeldstuen* (The Mountain Hut), with a folk-dance ballet; and a recital, with stage setting, by the renowned peasant fiddler Torgeir Audunsön or ' Myllargutten ' (' The Miller's Boy '), some of whose *slåtter* Grieg was to arrange for piano in his Op. 72. Bull's enthusiasm and personality combined with the fervour of the nationalist party to make this first season a successful one. The young Ibsen was appointed resident author and producer and a government grant was applied for. This, however, was not forthcoming; and Bull had to abandon his venture for the time being and set off once more for America, where he involved himself in another ill-fated scheme, later satirised in Ibsen's *Peer Gynt*: the foundation of a Norse colony to be called Oleana. When the Bergen theatre was reopened half a dozen years later it was Björnson who took over the office of artistic director, Ibsen having transferred his talents to Christiania.

Both these great dramatists were to be closely associated with Grieg's career. Björnson he seems to have met for the first time in Denmark in the summer of 1865; Ibsen in the following year at Rome. The three names are linked by an application Grieg made to Björnson, with Ibsen's support, for the post of musical director at the Christiania theatre of which Björnson had recently been made director.

Grieg failed to get the appointment; but Ibsen consoled him by saying he was reserved for something better than a Kapellmeister's post. In spite of this setback, Grieg had no stronger ally than Björnson in the early days of his career in the capital. The dramatist was looking for a new collaborator, for Nordraak, who had written incidental music for *Maria Stuart* and *Sigurd Slembe* and had been his partner in ambitious projects for a Norse opera, had just died at the age of twenty-three. Grieg was therefore swept up by the whirl-wind of Björnson's productivity. No occasion of civic or national importance was allowed to pass without its ode, hymn or cantata; and although Grieg, always a diffident and spasmodic composer, found it hard to keep up the pace, he profited from the friendly discipline and gained encouragement from Björnson's reliance on him. Their first important act of collaboration, the cantata *Foran Sydens Kloster*, is noticed in the next chapter; it was followed by the production of the historical drama *Sigurd Jorsalfar* (Sigurd the Crusader), with incidental music by Grieg.

The play is based on an episode in the Heimskringla Saga. During the earlier part of the twelfth century Norway was ruled by two brothers, one of whom, Eystejn or Öistein, kept the country in good order, while the other, Sigurd, took part in a crusade to the Holy Land. The action of Björnson's play deals with a quarrel between the kings over Borghild, daughter of Olav of Dale, and a dispute between their bands of followers as to which of the two kings has done more for the welfare and honour of the people. A reconciliation is brought about and the play closes with a song in praise of both brothers. This is the *Kongekvad* which, together with the war-song *Norröna-Folket, der vil fare!*, Grieg set for tenor or baritone solo with male voice chorus. The two pieces are in the square-cut, forth-right style best known outside Norway from Nordraak's setting of *Ja, vi elsker*, the Norwegian national anthem, though it probably owes its origin to Kjerulf's part-songs for male voices and the stage choruses of J. P. E. Hartmann. Part of the melody of Grieg's *Kongekvad* is given as Ex. 65 to show its quasi-modal character.

All five numbers of the *Sigurd* music were published in vocal-and-piano score by Lose of Copenhagen, as Op. 22, though later, in 1892, Grieg re-scored the three instrumental pieces and re-published them as an orchestral suite, Op. 56. The first of these three movements, now known as the ' Introduction ', was originally used as the prelude to the Second Act of the play; it was adapted, however, from a salon piece for violin and piano which Grieg had written in 1869 and which he was to play, with the violinist Johannes Wolf, before Queen Victoria in 1897. In *Sigurd Jorsalfar* it was called *Ved Mandjaevningen*, which denotes the ' matching-game ' described in the saga and in Björnson's dialogue. In an attempt to amuse the company and arouse his brother from his morose humour, Eystejn begins the traditional pastime of comparing the deeds and virtues of two prominent people—in this case, his brother and himself. The game develops into bitter strife between the warriors seated at the feasting-tables. The Intermezzo (Borghild's Dream) is the prelude to the second part of Act I. Björnson's stage direction runs : ' Before the curtain goes up, soft music begins, and during the rise of the curtain depicts her (Borghild's) dream, until it mounts to a pitch of great anguish; she cries out, wakes, and rises. The music reflects her awakening, confused thoughts. . . .' From further indications in the scene it would appear that Björnson had wanted ' background music ' during a considerable part of Borghild's soliloquy, but Grieg brings the music to an end before Borghild speaks. Her disquiet and remorse are suggested in the opening theme of the prelude (Ex. 66). This is soon combined with another theme introduced by violins and transformed in the middle section of the movement into an allegro agitato. The third piece in the *Sigurd* suite is the well-known *Homage March* accompanying the entry of the two kings and their retainers in Act III, after their reconciliation. The opening fanfare is an addition made to the original march when it was prepared for concert performance. The main theme is first given out softly by four solo 'cellos (see Ex. 16), and the tempo marking is Molto moderato e nobile, not Allegretto marziale as in the concert version. A fresh motive (bassoon and tuba; poco a poco animato) marks the entry of the halberdiers, who range themselves on the steps leading to the twin thrones. At this point Grieg inserted twelve additional bars in 1892; the trio of the march, which is closely akin to the trio of the tempo di minuetto in the Piano Sonata, was another addition made for concert performance—as was, of course, the repeat of the main section.

The first performance of *Sigurd Jorsalfar* took place on Independence Day, May 17, 1872. Both dramatist and composer were present and were called on to the stage at the end of the evening, though Grieg had suffered torments from the attempt of one of the principal actors to sing his part in the *Kongekvad* that closes the play.[1]

Another of the fruits of Grieg's collaboration with Björnson must be noticed at this point, as although it hardly comes into the category of stage music it was conceived on dramatic lines. In spite of one or two successful modern examples, melodrama is regarded with disfavour by present-day music-lovers; but it enjoyed a long run of popularity during the nineteenth century, and was employed by many of the major composers of the period from Beethoven and Weber to Richard Strauss. Grieg's model for his melodrama *Bergljot* was probably the first of Liszt's works in this form, *Lenore* (ballad by Bürger), published in 1860. Grieg composed *Bergljot* in 1871 but did not orchestrate it until 1885, when it received its first performance with the actress Laura Gundersen speaking the verses. Björnson's poem is again founded on an episode from the Heimskringla Saga. King Harald Hårdråde has treacherously put to death Ejnar, a powerful leader of the bönder (peasant proprietors), and his son Ejndride. 'When Bergljot, Ejnar Tambarskjelve's wife, who had remained in the hostelry of the town, heard of the deaths of her husband and son, she went straightaway up to the king's palace, where the bönder army was assembled, and egged them on to fight. But at that very moment the king was rowing down the river. Then said Bergljot: "Now lack we my friend Håkon Ivarson; Ejnar's killer should never row downstream if Håkon stood by the river bank"'.

Grieg's music begins with a brief fanfare. The speaker then describes how Bergljot, hearing the sound of voices and seeing the dust of a marching host, thinks that her husband and the bönder must be joined with Harald in conflict. She summons her chariot to carry her into the midst of the battle. All this is declaimed in detached phrases backed by tremolandos on lower strings and soft drum-rolls, with horn and trumpet calls increasing in urgency. A resolute theme (Ex. 67) comes to the fore as Bergljot calls upon the bönder to protect Ejnar. But the followers of Harald escape to their ships while the people stand in horror around the two corpses. A short, restless figure (Ex. 68) depicts Bergljot's agitation. As she realises the truth, the horns begin a poignant but restrained lament

---

[1] Grieg's setting of Björnson's *Landkjaenning* was also given its first performance on this date, at a bazaar in aid of the fund for the restoration of Trondhjem Cathedral.

(Ex. 69); this is repeated with fuller instrumentation, and Bergljot bewails the loss of her husband and son. But soon her mood again changes; she calls upon the people to avenge her, while the music rises to a climax of despair at the words, ' O, stood he here, Håkon Ivarson! '

Up to this point the verse has been declaimed in free speech rhythm against a musical background; but now musical rhythm and dynamics take control. After a five-bar prelude Bergljot's lamentation drops gradually into the underlying musical pattern, until every syllable is being uttered with accurate duration and metrical accent. This effective change enhances the saga-like dignity of the verse, and at the same time makes the musical setting more of an organic unity. Bergljot invokes ' the new god ' to avenge her, and then the funeral procession begins. The timpani, tuned to the perfect fourth GC, maintain a crotchet-beat ostinato, the double-basses reiterate an arpeggio figure of their own (Ex. 70), and within the space of little more than fifty bars Grieg builds up an impression of tragic grandeur worthy of Björnson's fine lines, with their often-quoted culmination :

> Kjör langsomt: Ti sådan körte Ejnar altid;—
> og vi kommer tidsnok hjaem.

> (Drive slowly, for so was Ejnar wont to drive,
> and soon enough we shall reach home.)

Among the subjects Björnson had suggested to Nordraak as being suitable for an opera was the story of Olav Trygvason, one of the most romantic figures in Norse history. Olav spent his youth in Sweden, Esthonia, and Russia; sailed to England on a Viking expedition and there became a Christian; settled for a time in Ireland; and returned to Norway to supplant the unpopular Jarl Haakon. Ascending the throne in 995, he compelled his subjects to accept Christianity. Although his methods of spreading the Gospel were hardly in accordance with its teachings, Olav has been given much credit for his missionary zeal and was a particular hero of nineteenth-century writers; Longfellow, it will be remembered, wrote a *Saga of King Olaf* on which Elgar was to base one of his early cantatas. Björnson too adopted the romantic attitude to Olav, or at least we can assume that his treatment of the subject would have been of that order had he completed the drama. But he wrote no more than the first three scenes, so that for our knowledge of how the action was to develop we have to rely partly upon some remarks made by Nina Grieg in

G

the year after her husband's death, partly upon a letter from the author himself.

Björnson seems to have begun *Olav Trygvason* in 1872. In July of the following year he sent Grieg the first three scenes with a characteristically exuberant note promising the remainder of the work and urging Grieg to have the whole opera ready by the following October. Grieg not unnaturally wanted a synopsis of the plot, or at least to know how the opening scenes were to be related to the whole drama. But Björnson had already gone off on a fresh tack; he had begun in the same year to interest himself in writing plays about contemporary life and manners, such as *Redaktören* (The Editor) and *En Fallit* (A Bankruptcy), which in some ways ran on parallel lines to the experiments Ibsen was making at the same period. It is therefore not surprising that Björnson found it difficult to drag himself back to historical drama and complete *Olav Trygvason*; what was less reasonable was his fury with Grieg for undertaking *Peer Gynt* in the summer of 1874, thereby shelving *Olav* for what Björnson took to be another opera text. The unedifying dispute dragged on for several years, dramatist and composer accusing each other of procrastination and negligence. But Björnson never sent another line, and Grieg abandoned the work as an opera, letting the sketches lie in his desk until the end of 1889, when he adapted them for concert performance. This cause of estrangement between the two friends led, happily, to an opportunity for reconciliation when Grieg dedicated the concert version of *Olav* to Björnson in warm and generous terms.

The setting of the three extant scenes of *Olav Trygvason* is an ancient Norse temple. The people, led by a high priest and a völva or prophetess, are invoking the counsel of the gods on the approach of Olav and his 'new gods, strange gods'. The völva, after carving runes to control the evil spirits, prophesies that Olav will enter the temple; 'Come he unscathed out, then will we believe!' The people thank the gods for their message. High priest and elders march round the sacred fires carrying the ceremonial horns, and then the ritual games begin, with leaping over the fires, a round dance for men and women, and a sword-dance. This brings us to the end of the third scene, and (as we have seen) to the end of the libretto as the author left it. According to Nina Grieg, the first act was to conclude with a scene in which the high priest's daughter, left behind in the deserted temple, is about to close the doors when she is suddenly confronted by the tremendous figure of Olav standing in dazzling armour on the threshold. Involuntarily she sinks to her knees before him. The curtain falls. As for the remainder of the drama, Björnson himself described the final scene as a tableau; the pagan temple has been destroyed, and Olav stands by its ruins, surrounded by a white-robed throng awaiting baptism. The conception is a thoroughly Norwegian one in its abrupt, vivid contrasts of mood and colour, and the author's failure to carry it out completely must be a matter for regret. Writing in 1886[1] of his admiration for Wagner's *Tristan* and *Parsifal* he adds: ' Now you will realise why I often go out and stare up at the clouds as if I could find there the Norwegian drama in Norwegian music which I have dreamt of, which I have always believed I could create some day, but which I now begin to think is fated to come from another.'

Scanty though the materials are for an assessment of Grieg's potentialities as an operatic writer, the completed scenes of *Olav* are interesting enough in the light they throw on the composer's reactions to the prevailing Wagnerian outlook of his time. We know something of this from another source. During 1876 Grieg visited Bayreuth, heard *The Ring*, and sent home to *Bergensposten* a set of articles dealing critically with Wagner's music and his theories. In particular he attacks Wagner's treatment of the voice in the many passages in his later works where it is subordinated in power and also in interest to the orchestral texture, and complains of the ungratefulness of so much of Wagner's vocal writing. We are reminded of these strictures when we open the score of *Olav*; for it is clear that Grieg has been at pains to work out his own system of declamation, balancing musical and dramatic considerations, and striving to bring out the individuality of the Norwegian language.

Sensitiveness to the diction, phrasing, and intonation of their own languages is one of the chief means by which non-German composers were able to assert their independence during the heat of the Wagnerian summer. Mussorgsky in Russia (as Monrad-Johansen points out, *Boris* is almost exactly contemporary with *Olav Trygvason*), Smetana in Bohemia, Verdi in Italy, Sullivan in England, and later, Debussy in France, all showed distinction in treating their native speech musically. The whole subject of the relationship between language and musical style has up to now received little attention, especially in relation to the nationalist schools of the nineteenth century. It would be interesting, for example, to study the extent to which the strongly-marked tones of spoken Norwegian

[1] Letter to Frants Beyer, August 27.

are reproduced in the vocal music of Grieg and other Norwegian composers, and to consider how far such a passage as Ex. 71, taken from *Olav Trygvason*, might be regarded as a stylisation of tone-inflected speech. Whatever the validity of the theory I have tentatively suggested, there can be no doubt about the effectiveness of the passage. The combination of monotone, rising augmented fourth, and, in the choral ejaculations, the falling perfect fifth, is at once realistic and uncanny. The tritone in particular is exploited to produce all the *diablerie* attributed to it in medieval times. Grieg was to make use of much the same effect in the scene with the sæter-girls in *Peer Gynt*.

The high priest's sentences are contrasted with those of one of the women worshippers, who calls upon the goddess Frigga in phrases that partake of the character of recitative while remaining essentially lyrical (Ex. 72). The sign-manual of Grieg's harmonic style will be observed in the above example, with its combination of highly chromatic harmonies and pedal notes. Generally, the chorus parts in this first scene are broadly and effectively diatonic, with an occasional inclination towards modality and much unison writing; it is only towards the close of the scene that the influence of Meyerbeer and Wagner is felt.

In the second scene, with the völva's incantation and prophecy, the 'runic' atmosphere is maintained by the use of monotone, perfect fifths, and octaves in the vocal line. The chorus again makes a powerful contribution. This scene culminates in the völva's oracular utterance, the people sing their hymn of thanksgiving to the gods, and the high priest blesses the sacred horns.

It was in the third scene, devoted to the ritual games, that Grieg was accused of plagiarising from *Carmen*. We know, from a letter written in 1905, how greatly he admired Bizet's work though in the same place he expresses the wish that he had known *Carmen* thirty years before. Grieg had a notoriously bad memory for dates and facts, but he can hardly have seen *Carmen* (first performed in Paris on March 3, 1875) before writing *Olav*. It is more tempting to look for echoes of Bizet in the exotic scenes of *Peer Gynt*, and also perhaps more permissible on grounds of date. But even if Grieg had to wait until 1905 (when Peters sent him the score) to get to know *Carmen*, he might well have come across earlier works of Bizet's: *Djamileh*, perhaps, with its Oriental colouring, or *Les Pêcheurs de Perles*.

But it is not *Carmen* we think of and compare with the temple dance scene in *Olav* so much as a work of considerably later date:

Prince Igor. Grieg's choral dances fall very far short of the *élan* and barbaric colour of the Polovtsian episodes, though there are interesting parallels such as the opening of the final section (presto) of Grieg's scene which curiously foreshadows the boys' dance in *Prince Igor.* But in spite of the comparative lack of rhythmic enterprise in *Olav* there are occasional touches of the genuine and inimitable Grieg magic (cf. Ex. 73).

Olav Trygvason is not exportable; Björnson has seen to that by treating his subject with a wealth of antiquarian imagery and allusion that make it incomprehensible to audiences ignorant of the byways of northern mythology; nor, as we have seen, does the work in its incomplete state offer any concessions to those who look for human characterisation. Its main interest to the world at large is as an historical document, showing a facet of the many-sided romantic and nationalistic movement in nineteenth-century music.

It has been said that one of the reasons why *Olav Trygvason* was never completed was that Ibsen commissioned what Grieg described as ' a few fragments ' of incidental music for *Peer Gynt.* Grieg's first contact with Ibsen had been in Rome in 1866, when they discussed plans for an opera to be based on Ibsen's *Olav Liljekrans.* It was Grieg's fate to be haunted throughout his life by the ghosts of unwritten operas. As late as 1893 we find him again shrinking from a proposal—again emanating from Ibsen—for an adaptation of *Haermændene på Helgeland* (The Warriors in Helgeland). But *Peer Gynt* was, from the points of view of author and composer alike, a brilliant success. The two orchestral suites, which Grieg afterwards drew from his music, did more than anything else to make his reputation abroad as an orchestral composer; while Ibsen had the generosity to make public acknowledgment of the service Grieg had done him in tempering the chill blast of his northern muse to the shorn lamb that was the average European theatre-goer of the 'eighties. Whether Grieg's music is altogether in keeping with conditions of the modern stage is a more debatable point, one producer at least having declared his wish ' to jettison Grieg, to jettison any realistic scenery; and to spend the time thus saved on playing more of the text than is otherwise possible. For *Peer Gynt* is not a naturalistic any more than it is an operatic piece '. In further, and more detailed criticisms of the dramatic propriety of Grieg's score, the same writer[1] shows imperfect acquaintance

---

[1] Tyrone Guthrie, in his Foreword to *Peer Gynt.* English version by Norman Ginsbury (London, 1945).

with the music, and more especially with the effect Grieg and Ibsen wanted it to make; but there is something in his contention that ' certain scenes are given undue weight and importance by the music '.

It is hardly necessary to point out that the two *Peer Gynt* concert suites are an insufficient basis for estimating the range and variety of Grieg's contribution to the original stage production. The ' few fragments ' (about twenty in all) gathered together in the full score published posthumously show that Grieg revelled in the opportunities for Norwegian colouring provided by the first and last sections of the drama, responded less originally and consistently in the Oriental scenes—Anitra's dance suggests Copenhagen rather than Cairo—and failed to produce anything much above the level of the hack theatre-composer in those places where Ibsen prescribed melodrama. On the whole, however, the music is successful in creating a variety of back-grounds, in heightening dramatic situations, and in bringing out the folklore elements on which setting and diction are so often based. It is Grieg who helps to make Ibsen's swift transitions of mood and scene intelligible to the spectator or listener (the reader is, naturally, in a more independent position) and when all is said and done, heightens the poetical aspect of the drama, whether in the bucolic festivities that open the play, or the wild sensuality of the sæter-girls, or the bizarrerie of the Troll-scenes, or the fantastic and poignant episode of Aase's death, or the tourist's Orient in the African scenes, or the storm at sea in the last act (an obvious debt to Wagner), or the supernatural voices that accuse Peer, or the devotion of Solveig as expressed in her songs. Aimar Grönvold once pointed out that strongly-marked contrasts are among the most characteristic features of Norwegian art. It is certainly through contrasts that Grieg often obtains his most telling effects as, for example, when he begins the prelude to Act II of *Peer Gynt* by bringing two short phrases into juxtaposition, one suggesting the impetuosity of Peer's behaviour, the other dropping a hint of baleful and unseen forces at work (Ex. 74). This antithesis is repeated, and Ingrid's lament then follows: a sweeping melody full of the most intense passion and making, with its broadly-phrased structure, yet another element of contrast. At the close of the lament a kettledrum solo leads abruptly into a double repetition of the short contrasting motives already described. Altogether this is one of Grieg's most original and poetic movements.

The composer himself distinguished such highly-expressive

passages as the foregoing, the highly-charged music for muted strings that accompanies the scene of Aase's death, Solveig's songs, the *Morning Mood* that forms the prelude to the first African scene, and some less-known pieces, such as the interesting short prelude for strings and horns, prophetic of Sibelius, that precedes the Fourth Act, from those parts of the drama where ' there was no question of music '. In the latter he is content to underline Ibsen's dramatic effects by the reiteration, often sequential, of simple but striking motives, and by vivid colouring. The scene of Peer's encounter with the sæter-girls is a good example; the rising fourths of the girls' voices, so strongly resembling the ritual chants in *Olav Trygvason*, are set against a background of string tremolandos in open fourths and fifths (Ex. 75). It was of this scene that Grieg wrote to Hennum, conductor at the Christiania Theatre, before the first performance in 1876 :

> This is a dangerous piece, which will either make a really bad effect or an absolutely splendid one, wild and devilish and sensual, all according to how the participants *sing* and *act*. Here is precisely one of those places where I think the music ceases to be music. . . . Of course you will have a bad time with the singing, because prima donnas *ex professo* account it beneath their dignity to sing such stuff, as they don't gather any laurels thereby, and actresses, I suppose, haven't the vocal resources. But there must be life in it—that's the main thing!

The music of this scene as we now know it is the result of a revision Grieg carried out in 1885, when the work was revived at Copenhagen. Grieg was never quite at home with the orchestra (except perhaps its string section) and was continually touching up his scores, so that up to the time of his death there was no complete and authentic score of *Peer Gynt* in print. Grieg's orchestration, though rarely adventurous, is more enterprising in this work than elsewhere. Piano, xylophone, harp and cowbell are introduced into the dance of the Dovre-King's daughter, a movement which the composer intended as ' an absolute parody '; tambourines and other quasi-Oriental instruments make their appearance in the Arabian dance; the organ is heard in the litany-like passages in Act V.

Although the two *Peer Gynt* suites are among the most hackneyed works in the concert repertory most of the remaining numbers are comparatively little known, and as the full score is at present almost inaccessible, a summary of its contents may be useful for reference :

1. *Prelude to Act I. I Bryllupsgården* (At the Wedding). This supplies local colouring and introduces fragments of Solveig's song and of the dances (halling and springdans) which are heard on a solo viola played behind the scenes.
2. *Brudefölget drager forbi* (Wedding March), orchestrated by Halvorsen from Grieg's *Pictures of Folk Life* (Op. 19, No. 2).
3. *Halling* and *Springdans,* for the wedding scene; played off-stage by a solo violin, with ornaments and double-stopping in imitation of the traditional style of the Hardanger-fiddle.
4. *Prelude to Act II.* The Bride-rape, and Ingrid's lament. Included in the second suite.
5. *Peer Gynt and the Sæter-Girls.* Set to music throughout, except for Peer's lines which are spoken as melodrama.
6. *Close of the Scene with the Green-clad Woman.* Peer rides off on the boar's back (a few bars of grotesque music).
7. *In the Hall of the Dovre-King.* The well-known movement included in the first suite, but with the chorus parts in accordance with Ibsen's direction : ' The older trolls sing, the young ones dance.' Ends abruptly with the King's command: ' Ice in your blood! ' [1]
8. *Dance of the Dovre-King's Daughter.* Described by the composer as a parody. Interesting as an experiment in the bizarre, with use of modal melody and harmony.
9. *Peer Hunted by the Trolls.* Melodrama, the music (Ex. 76) based on a transformation of the theme of No. 7. Ends with the ringing of the church-bells and the flight of the trolls. Continuous with :
9b. *Scene with the Böjg.* Melodrama with chorus representing bird-voices. Ends with the distant sound of bells and organ from the church in the valley.
10. *Prelude to Act III.* A short, sombre piece for strings and horns used antiphonally. (Composed at a later date.)
11. *Solveig's Song.* Orchestral version, to be played as a prelude to the third scene if scene-shifting makes this necessary. Included in the second suite.
12. *The Death of Aase.* For muted strings, as in first suite.
13. *Prelude to Act IV. Morgenstemning* (Morning Mood). Originally meant to introduce the fifth scene of this act—hence its sub-title. Included in first suite.
14. *The Thief and the Receiver.* Act IV, Scene 5; set as a miniature operatic scene for two bass voices.
15. *Arabian Dance.* Included in second suite. Stage version has an optional chorus of women's voices, with a solo part when Anitra dances alone.
16. *Anitra's Dance.* Included in first suite. For strings and triangle alone. Described as tempo di mazurka.

[1] According to Grieg's letter to Beyer of December 22, 1885, this scene was to be extended at the Copenhagen revival to include a ballet to the *Norwegian Dances*, Op. 35, specially orchestrated for the occasion.

17. *Peer Gynt's Serenade*. From Act IV, Scene 7.
18. *Solveig's Song*. First sung version, with accompaniment for flutes, clarinets and muted strings.
19. *Prelude to Act V*. Peer Gynt's homecoming, Represents a stormy evening off the coast of Norway, and the shipwreck.
20. *Solveig's Song*. Second version, unaccompanied.
21. *Scene at Night, on the Heath*. Melodrama, with chorus accompanied by organ and representing dead leaves, dewdrops, broken straws. Closes with the voice of Aase and the final bars from the music of her death-scene.
22. *Chorale*, sung by the congregation on the way to Whitsun service.
23. *Solveig's Lullaby*. Accompanied by harp and strings. This closes the drama.[1]

---

[1] For a fuller account of the composition of Grieg's *Peer Gynt* music see *Music and Letters*, Vol. XXVI, No. 2, April 1945. The earlier published versions often differ from the final one: thus ' The Death of Aase ' was originally in A minor, adagio, instead of in B minor, andante doloroso, and had no dynamic marking louder than *p*; bars 25–32 were inserted later. ' In the Hall of the Dovre-King ' originally began without the F sharps of the horns; ' Anitra's Dance ' ended with a fortissimo chord; various cuts were made in the final version of ' Morning Mood '.

8

Choral Music

By

Edmund Rubbra

GRIEG LIVED AT A time when the real choral tradition had been almost overlaid by the seemingly more dramatic and dynamic possibilities of instrumental colour. In terms of texture, this meant that linear melodic writing had become secondary to harmony conceived as a vehicle for dramatic and lyrical outpourings. Thus, choral tone in the period we are discussing was considered as a legitimate extension of instrumental tone, rather than as a body of sound that, as in the sixteenth and seventeenth centuries, grew from purely vocal roots. This is not said in criticism of the later viewpoint as such, but criticism can be focused on the results of treating voices merely as other instruments in the general ensemble. When, in place of virile part-writing, which opens up endless possibilities in fluidity of harmony, the newest findings in chord structures (in Grieg's case various combinations of the ninth) are the focal points of the texture, the tendency is for the music to 'date' rather quickly, unless the juxtapositions and contexts of the harmonic structure are original, or there is an overriding virility of rhythm. This tendency is emphasised in choral music, because voices so perceptibly soften harmonic asperities. As against this criticism, one can point to a certain homogeneity of effect when the voices are accompanied by an orchestra, and in this connection it is curious to note that in Grieg's limited output of choral music that which is accompanied tends to be the more harmonically static, while the unaccompanied visibly expands to include contrapuntal elements. Indeed, in parts of *Hvad est du dog skjön* (How fair is Thy face), the first of the Psalms, Op. 74, for mixed voices, the colouristic harmonic world has been quite abandoned. In the unaccompanied works, too, there is a far greater rhythmic freedom and virility, gained from a deep familiarity with Scandinavian folk-song and folk-dance music. In general, it can be said that the orchestra when used by Grieg as an accompaniment to voices had a shackling effect, reducing the vocal part, however dramatic or lyrically moving, to an instrumental apanage, whereas in the choral music that had to be self-subsistent a much wider and further roaming personality comes to the fore.

Grieg's first published choral work is *Foran Sydens Kloster* (At a Southern Convent Gate), Op. 20, a setting of some words from Björnson's *Arnljot Gjelline*, that in the manner of condensed folk-tales proceeds by question and answer, the ' homeless maiden ' knocking at the cloister-door being subjected to exhaustive enquiry before it is established that her father was slain by her lover. She is then admitted, to the singing of a ' choir of nuns from the lighted church.' This latter is the only choral section in the work, all the previous four verses being set for soprano and alto soli, with orchestral support. The work, composed in 1871, is dedicated to Liszt, whom Grieg met in Italy the year before, and it is not unfanciful to detect in its formal construction and in the somewhat frenzied chromatic writing in the orchestral part more than a trace of the influence of the older composer, although in the final nuns' chorus Grieg escapes the sentimentality with which Liszt would have invested the occasion. Altogether it is a finely expressive little work, that would be well worth reviving.

In the two songs for solo (baritone–tenor), male chorus and orchestra that form part of the *Sigurd Jorsalfar* music, as in Op. 20, the choral writing is not a very prominent feature : indeed, four-part writing is found only in the final bars of each of the two songs. The vocal line is direct, diatonic and of a popular cast (cf. Ex. 65) : the essential Grieg being found in the occasional sliding chromatic harmonies of the accompaniment, and in the choral ending of the second song (Exs. 77 and 78). Yet a personal imprint is found even in the most blatantly obvious diatonic passages (Ex. 79), making clear a fact often forgotten in any critical estimate of Grieg : that he was a composer whose craftsmanship, although engaged in a somewhat narrowly circumscribed field, was of a high order.

Op. 30, the *Album for Mandssang* (Album for Male Voices), is the first unaccompanied choral work of Grieg. Percy Grainger, who is responsible for the translations from Norwegian into English of this and other works of Grieg, says in his foreword that Grieg considered this *Album for Male Voices* (baritone solo, tenors and basses), all folk-song arrangements, as ' the most important of his choral compositions '. Certainly here Grieg's lovely and sensitive lyrical sense is seen to its greatest advantage. The melodic clashes (Exs. 80

and 81) are poignant and logical, and the reiteration of the word
' never ' (' ingen ' in the Norwegian) in the first setting *Jeg lagde mig
så sildig* (I laid me down to slumber)[1] with its shifting harmonies
has quite a Purcellian anguish (cf. the last few bars of *Dido and
Aeneas,* where Purcell treats the same word in a curiously similar
way). The second song is a delightful and picturesque *Bådn-Låt*
(Children's Song), a setting of words that, like most nursery rhymes,
are devoid of logical meaning. The rhythmic vocal accompaniment
of nonsense syllables (with a punctuating ' miaow ' from the tenor
soloist) is carried a stage further in the fourth of this set, *Kvaalin's
Halling,* a vocal and cumulative peasant dance where the voices
supporting the soloist are treated in an entirely instrumental-
rhythmic way. This and the last of these settings (*Rötnams-Knut*—
a familiar figure in Norwegian folk-song) are most successful
instances of musical onomatopœicism. One of the attractions of this
Album is its variety of content, a variety not gained at the expense
of simplicity. They are choral parallels to many of the perfectly
formed instrumental miniatures, and they should be known far more
widely. No. 5 is an ironical quasi-patter setting of words beginning
Dæ œ den störste Dårlehet (There is no folly half so great),[2] while
No. 6, *Går e ut ein Kveld* (When I take a stroll) (described as a
springdans), is in reality a virile drinking-song with some extra-
ordinarily effective contrary-motion thirds and sixths (Ex. 83). The
least successful are two of the ' religious ' settings, *Torö Liti* (Little
Thora) and *Den store, hvide Flok* (The Great White Host), which,
lacking the rhythmic drive of the others, tend to become harmonically mawkish.

Grieg's loyalty to Björnson is again illustrated by his next work, a
setting for baritone solo, male chorus and orchestra, of a poem called
Landkjaenning. This is usually somewhat clumsily translated as
' Recognition of Land ', giving the spiritual explorations of Olaf
Trygvason, the hero of the unfinished Björnson-Grieg opera
described in the previous chapter, an earthiness that is foreign to the
inner meaning of the original poem. Nor does Grieg eschew earthiness in his setting : indeed, it is heartily heroic, and goes forward with
a diatonic forcefulness, unrelieved by much subtlety of harmony,
except, maybe, in the section marked ' religioso ' (Ex. 84). But it is
precisely here that one of Grieg's besetting lapses is most in evidence :

---

[1] It must have been this melody (Ex. 82) that Grieg had in mind when he
composed Solveig's song, which was admittedly modelled on a folk-song.—ED.
[2] Grieg set another, very different variant of the same song for piano, as Op. 66,
No. 2.

that is, the unvaried repetition of a small harmonic sequence or phrase, as though love of the harmony or phrase *per se* had temporarily silenced formal demands.

By far the most important of Grieg's choral music are the settings of Four Psalms for unaccompanied mixed voices, Op. 74, ' free adaptations ' of old Norwegian Psalm-tunes. (These are said to be the last works that Grieg wrote.) It is remarkable how many composers in the course of development have gradually relied less and less upon a harmonic-romantic vocabulary and more and more upon the rarer ' ether ' of clear unclouded lines. Grieg was no exception to this, and although he has not in these last Psalms completely shaken off the too-easy acceptance of his own harmonic findings, we yet find a texture that has been amazingly clarified, revealing a skeletal hardness in place of a romantic flabbiness. There is, too, especially in the first, a quite medieval austerity and purity in the harmony (Ex. 85), an exceptionally imaginative treatment of cadences (Ex. 86), and at the climax of No. 1 (p. 7) a strikingly bold series of diatonic sequences. Notable also in No. 1 is the major feeling of the bass solo against the A minor tonality of the rest of the chorus, and the inversion of effect in the last verse, where the chorus is in A major and the solo line twisted towards the minor by flattening the leading note and the supertonic. The second Psalm has also a striking example of clashing tonalities, the baritone solo of the tranquillo section being in B flat major as against the B flat minor of the chorus (Ex. 102). Grieg has, of course, taken care that there should be no strident cacophony (as Holst did in his polytonal canons), yet the effect is successful and ingenious. In the third, *Jesus Kristus er opfaren* (Jesus Christ our Lord is risen) there is some lovely free melismatic writing, coupled again with a beautiful treatment of cadences, and if the earlier Grieg recurs in the final chromatic ' Kyrie ', it is so rooted in its tonality and so strong in its false relations that the effect is exhilarating. The fourth Psalm, *I Himmelen* (In Heaven above), has a touching simplicity, but a fine confident strength is shown in the climax to each verse, where the voices are poised on a fairly violent discord. I count this set of *Four Psalms* as among the finest choral music of the nineteenth century, and it should be far more widely known, not only for its intrinsic qualities, but because it reveals a facet of the composer that has remained largely unrecognised.

There is one other choral work (without opus number) available for study, an arrangement by Grieg of his song *Ave, Maris Stella*, for mixed chorus. It is an unimportant work, but has a charmingly lyrical naïveté and a few characteristic touches of harmony in the shape of what are known in harmony text-books as consecutive diatonic or secondary sevenths.

9

Musical Personality and Style

By

John Horton

I F IT IS TRUE THAT the greatest genius is the most indebted man, then the converse may equally be true : that conspicuous originality of technique or idiom is to be sought among artists of lesser calibre, or, to avoid irrelevant as well as invidious comparisons, among specialists. Genius in art asserts itself partly by its catholicity in extracting elements of all kinds from its antecedents and in transmuting those elements into new products that both fulfil and transcend the past. Palestrina, J. S. Bach, Handel, Haydn, Mozart, Beethoven, Wagner all mount upon the shoulders of their predecessors to heights never scaled before. But for fresh modes of musical speech, for novel colourings, for experimentation and exploration, we look rather to the Domenico Scarlattis, the C. P. E. Bachs, the Webers, the Chopins, the Glinkas, the Smetanas, and the Griegs. It is they and their like who enchant us—only for a brief spell, perhaps—with the unfamiliar, the exotic and the bizarre; while genius devotes its energies to convincing us anew of the vitality of age-old truths.

Among the innovating talents of music Grieg has his place. No stronger proof is needed of the individuality of his speech than the ease with which it can be imitated and parodied; those descending thirds, those chords of the seventh and ninth, those dotted rhythms and square phrases are gifts to the caricaturist. So, for that matter, are the accompaniment figures and melodic embellishments of Chopin; the pentatonic tunes of Dvořák; the consecutive fifths and sevenths of Debussy; and yet we recognise these things, even behind the exaggerations of caricature, as little more than what logicians call the inseparable accidents of personality. The trouble with mannerisms in art, as in personal behaviour, is that they conceal important aspects of character while helping to betray others. And although Grieg retained certain tricks of musical speech and gesture throughout his career, these should not be allowed to hide from us the gradual unfolding of a personality that went on behind them.

Uncharitable critics sometimes suggest that it is an advantage to a minor artist to be born in a country whose folk-music has not been systematically capitalised and exported. An artist born in Norway in the 1840's was, however, faced with rather a complicated set of circumstances. He would grow up to find himself expected to choose between two distinct cultural parties. The radical school, of which the highly romantic, fervidly national poet Wergeland came to be acknowledged as the leader, sought the salvation of Norwegian art in renewed contact with the life and traditions of the bönder or peasant proprietors, whose qualities the nationalists were engaged in bringing to the notice both of their own countrymen and of Europe in general; while the more conservative school, to which the poet Welhaven and the musician Kjerulf adhered, denied the expediency of breaking off the thread of artistic relations between Norway and the other Scandinavian countries, and thus, as they feared, ceasing to be borne along with the main currents of European civilisation. It was a hard decision for Grieg to make. He belonged by birth and early associations to the class of officials, merchants and professional men, with their predominantly Danish background; and it might have been predicted that he would follow the path already trodden by Gade, who superimposed a mildly Scandinavian colouring on a neutral background of diluted German romanticism; or at most that of Kjerulf, who had no objection to writing in a folk-idiom when he thought the subject called for it—as, for example, when he set the songs in Björnson's peasant novels—but refused to take 'all this Norwegian business' seriously. But a chain of circumstances was to divert Grieg's interests forcibly into another direction.

One of these circumstances was his unhappy career at the Leipzig Conservatoire, ever afterwards to be referred to with loathing. It is hard to believe that the teaching in that institution was quite as bad as Grieg always said it was, but there seems no doubt that much of it was of a hit-or-miss order, resembling nothing so much as the methods of Dotheboys Hall, though the Yorkshire students had this slight advantage over the Leipzig ones, that they were taught to spell C-L-E-A-N W-I-N-D-E-R before being sent away to do it. Grieg may have been exaggerating when he said that Reinecke ordered him to write a string quartet without giving any previous instruction in the technique of the medium; but his published G minor Quartet, Op. 27, goes far to bear out the accuracy of his recollection. It was one of his misfortunes to have passed through his studentship at a time when the classical forms had become derelict shells wherein the successors of Mendelssohn and Schumann made their habitations like so many little hermit crabs. Liszt's symphonic poems were scarcely dry on the paper when Grieg entered the Conservatoire, and his teachers can have known little about them. In the same year the fifteen-year-old boy heard a work of Wagner's for the first time, and was so strongly attracted by it that he returned for thirteen successive performances. The work was *Tannhäuser*. Nearly twenty years were to pass before Brahms could begin his regeneration of the symphony. It is not surprising, then, that Grieg left the Conservatoire with small understanding of the true nature of form. The same may be said of his contemporary, the English student Arthur Sullivan, who was likewise handicapped throughout his career by the inability to raise a satisfying structure without a framework of words. Both composers are at their best when setting their native languages: both are at their dullest in such things as the *Autumn* and *In Memoriam* overtures, which they attempt to build around themes of song-like character. And yet Leipzig gave both of them an inordinate respect for the classical forms as such, and poor Grieg was to court an Æsopian disaster in trying to inflate his lyrical substance to symphonic dimensions. Even as late as 1877 he was expressing his determination to ' fight his way through the larger forms ', and only ten years later than that did he abandon the struggle, after the completion of the third Violin Sonata.

And yet the real crisis of his career had come, and the decision been taken, shortly after his departure from the Leipzig Conservatoire and his northward flight, like that of some migratory bird, to a haven where he might ' find expression for something of the best in himself, which lay a thousand miles away from Leipzig and its atmosphere '. He found what he sought, not in Norway, but in Copenhagen, that wholly charming centre of Scandinavian art and letters. At Copenhagen Gade reigned, secure in his memories of Mendelssohn's friendship and in his own title to leadership of the Scandinavian school. On learning that Grieg had only a few small piano pieces and songs to his name, Gade showed himself true to the principles of Leipzig and Mr. Squeers by bidding him go home and write a symphony. The work so commissioned was actually completed; but the title-page of the autograph bears the inscription : ' Never to be performed. E. G.' A year or so later, and again in Copenhagen, another meeting took place that was positive in its effect. Rikard Nordraak is one of those prophets who are without honour except in their own country. Such specimens of his compositions as are at present accessible lead one to suppose that his influence on Grieg was by far his greatest creative achievement; indeed, Grieg himself admitted that Nordraak's talents were not primarily those of a musician. But one can understand what refreshment Grieg must have gained from delicately-scented wild flowers like Nordraak's settings of verses by Björnson (who devoured young composers with the appetite of a fairy-tale giant, and to whom Nordraak was as the apple of his eye); for instance, *I skogen smågutten gik dagenlang* (The little boy went in the woods all day) (Ex. 87). Here we have already some features derived from folk-music, though often popularly thought to be mannerisms peculiar to Grieg and his imitators. The trochaic rhythm is there, the repetition of small melodic figures, the use of sequences and echoes (corresponding to the traditional forms of ballad poetry), the mixture of major and minor tonalities, the suggestion of modal influences and particularly of the mixolydian mode (see the final cadence of the vocal part), the falling seventh of the minor scale, the harmonisation on pedals. Nordraak completed what Ole Bull had begun; he awoke in Grieg realisation of the possibilities of what was in its way a highly developed art and, yet more important to a young Norseman still half stifled by the 'Leipzig atmosphere', a living and breathing art. He opened to Grieg a way of release, he gave him an impulse towards self-development. Could that keen wind from the snow-mountains bring to life the dry bones of those 'larger forms' that lay so heavily on his conscience? At least Grieg would begin at once to discharge his debt to Nordraak by writing the *Humoresques*, Op. 6—the first of his works to be written with intent (if one may Anglicise the German verb coined in derision of Grieg) to 'Norwegise', though still earlier works, notably the *Poetic Tone Pictures*, Op. 3, had shown a tendency towards a distinctively northern idiom, particularly in No. 5 of the set, where bare fourths and fifths, boldly superimposed and moving to a vigorous dance rhythm, burst unceremoniously into the *salon*.

Henceforward 'Norwegising' was to play an increasingly stronger part in the formation of Grieg's style, blending with other elements to produce a highly personal idiom. What those other elements were is worth considering. Chief among them, I think, are the influences of two composers whom Grieg learnt to admire in his childhood: Mozart and Chopin. 'Excepting Bach,' he wrote in a magazine article in 1897, '. . . no one has understood as well as Mozart how to use the chromatic scale to express the highest effect in music.' His Mozart was, in the main, the Mozart of the G minor String

Quintet ('Note,' he says, 'the wonderful chromatics of the first theme'), of the G minor Piano Quartet, and of the D minor Piano Concerto.[1] And his Chopin was the Chopin of the mazurkas, glowing with harmonic colour and alive with the rhythms of the Polish peasantry. From these two Grieg caught some of the magic of their use of the chromatic scale, with its power to turn the hearer adrift on unknown waters at some moment when he thinks himself to be wrapped in diatonic security. Grieg naturally came closer to Chopin in human sympathy, for their ideals were in many ways the same; both were passionately devoted to folk-music, both sought to assimilate it to a style already partly formed by cosmopolitan influences, both were primarily keyboard composers, achieving their best work when the piano was the whole or the main part of the medium, both were true harmonists in that they concentrated with intense interest on the chord as an entity, adjusting not only its essential intervals but also its balance and distribution of notes to obtain a nicely-calculated effect, both were weak in constructive power and generally failed when attempting to write on a broad scale. We shall have occasion to note further points of contact between the two composers, but the reader who wishes to observe the strength of Chopin's general influence on Grieg's earlier style may care to turn up some of the *Lyric Pieces*, such as Op. 12, No. 5 (*Folkevise*), Op. 38, No. 3 (*Melodie*), and No. 6 (*Elegie*); or the *Stemninger*, Op. 73—No. 5 of which is an étude with the sub-title *Hommage à Chopin*.

The earlier piano pieces and songs show, as one might expect, Leipzig influences too—Schumann, rather than Mendelssohn; and also Gade, a comparison of whose Piano Sonata in E minor with Grieg's in the same key (one of the first-fruits of his meeting with Nordraak) warms one's heart with affection for the enthusiasm and independent attitude of the young Norseman, if not for his Sonata. Unlike Nordraak, however, Grieg was no radical. He was too closely identified with Danish artistic society to throw overboard its traditions and ideals; to the end of his days he felt drawn towards bright, good-humoured and civilised Copenhagen rather than towards the capital of his own country, whose indifference to cultural values he never ceased to lament. Paradoxically it was in Denmark that Grieg began to 'Norwegise'; but he retained, until late in his career, a

---

[1] Grieg's affection for Mozart was considerably deeper than his feeling for Mozart's style, if we may judge by his additional piano parts to four of the master's piano sonatas.—ED.

115

well-defined 'Danish' style, elegant, charming and polished, to which he reverted on all sorts of occasions : not only in the Andersen songs, and in the *Holberg* Suite, written expressly to create the atmosphere of the comedies of 'the Molière of the North', but also in Anitra's dance in *Peer Gynt* and in many of the *Lyric Pieces*.

The Danish artistic temperament, of which Grieg had so large a share, was really more closely in sympathy with that of the French race than the German, in spite of much traffic with the latter. It had been so even in the seventeenth century, when Holberg (like Grieg, a Norwegian from Bergen) had been able to model his Danish comedies of manners on those of the Frenchman Molière. It is hardly too fanciful to attribute partly to French influence certain elements of Grieg's keyboard style; his love of *agréments*, for example, often reminds us of the clavecinists, although Grieg himself would probably have regarded them as derived partly from Schumann, partly from the traditional ornamentation of the peasant fiddle players. In his song-writing, too, Grieg leans towards French ideals rather than German; some of his happiest achievements in this field are, with their finish and delicacy of draughtmanship and avoidance of emotional excess, closer to the *chanson* than the *lied*. Even his harmonic language often has a Gallic flavour, again calling up associations with Couperin and his contemporaries (Ex. 88).

This spiritual relationship between Grieg and French music was by no means one-sided. The French were always among the warmest admirers of his music, and although Grieg's attitude in the Dreyfus affair and Debussy's depreciatory remarks about the Piano Concerto and other early works caused a considerable degree of estrangement at one period, the younger impressionists were impressed by his harmonic innovations and hailed the *Slåtter* with particular delight as an example of *le nouveau Grieg*. Ravel went so far as to say that he had scarcely written anything that was not influenced by Grieg; and, although this remark has been generally interpreted as polite flattery (Ravel was on a visit to Norway when he made it), we do well to remind ourselves that Debussy himself was only four years old (and Ravel minus nine!) when Grieg was writing such passages as Ex. 89 in his *March in memory of Nordraak* (dated April 6, 1866).

Nordraak's death occurred in the same year that Grieg left the congenial artistic climate of Copenhagen to take up his duties amid the rigours of the Norwegian capital. His isolation was almost complete when, two years later, he lost another ally, who, if much less passionately devoted to the nationalist cause, was probably the most gifted and sensitive composer Norway had so far produced. The songs and piano pieces of Halfdan Kjerulf, after enjoying a wave of popularity a generation or two ago, are now almost forgotten in this country; regrettably so, for some of them are distinctive and charming, besides being of considerable interest in relation to the works of Grieg. Kjerulf, like Nordraak and later Grieg himself, collaborated fairly extensively with the writer Björnson, and it is in his settings of lyrics from Björnson's folk-novels that his finished artistry combines with a feeling for national colour to produce some beautiful miniatures. It is difficult to believe that Kjerulf's setting of *Nu tak for alt* from Björnson's *Synnöve Solbakken* (Ex. 90) was entirely out of Grieg's mind when, six years after the death of Kjerulf, he composed Solveig's song in *Peer Gynt*. It is equally interesting to compare the two composers' settings of *Prinsessen* (Grieg's was written in 1871). A great deal of the similarity between Kjerulf's ' Norwegian ' style and Grieg's is naturally accounted for by their indebtedness to a common source : Norwegian folk-music, as collected and arranged by the celebrated organist Lindeman in the monumental work—*Aeldre og nyere fjeldmelodier*—that first came into Grieg's hands in 1869, though the first draft of it had been published in 1841, early enough for Kjerulf to have been influenced by it. Lindeman's arrangements, while simple enough for the domestic pianist to strum over, contrive not only to suggest much of the atmosphere of the originals, but also to add musicianly touches in the form of counterpoints, canonic imitations, and varied basses, and it is easy to see that Grieg must have obtained many hints from them when laying out material of folk character for the piano (cf. Ex. 91; Lindeman's and Grieg's harmonisations of the same melody have already been shown side by side in Ex. 57). Lindeman's collection certainly awoke in Grieg a fuller realisation of the wealth of Norwegian folk-music and poetry, and resulted in his exploring it still further in its natural state. We shall examine later some of the technical details he took over from folk-music.

David Monrad-Johansen, Grieg's most recent and comprehensive biographer, has made a penetrating analysis of the causes of Grieg's recurrent fits of depression, lack of artistic productivity, and sense of frustration which contrast so remarkably with the outwardly brilliant success of his later career as executant and composer. One cause I have already referred to : the stoniness of the soil on which he attempted to rear the delicate flower of his talent, and his unfor-

tunate isolation due to loss of most of the friends who might have
helped him with their sympathy or even through friendly rivalry.
Nordraak and Kjerulf, as we have seen, both died before 1870.
Svendsen migrated to Denmark in 1872. Eight years later Ole Bull,
after many wanderings about the world, came home to Norway to
die. Apart from the early Copenhagen days, when Grieg made
common cause with a group of young Danish musicians and helped
found the Euterpe society, he never had a strong backing of fellow-
enthusiasts of commensurate gifts. In this respect his position was
very different from that of the Russian nationalists, who not only
helped one another with mutual advice and criticism, but also had
the tremendous advantage of a common artistic parentage in Glinka,
a man of talent approaching genius. A comparison between Grieg
and the 'mighty handful' indeed suggests further difficulties that
beset the lonely Norseman. Ole Bull had dreamed of founding a
Norse Theatre in Bergen, the birthplace of Holberg, Welhaven and
Grieg, as a home for indigenous drama, opera, ballet and concert
music. Of these only the first grew up and flourished. On Norwegian
soil, as on British, opera was never more than a shy, sickly plant;
whereas the Russians, even before Glinka drove in the firm founda-
tions of a national opera, had a vigorous, though Italianate, operatic
tradition (as also a rich heritage of church music) fostered by imperial
patronage, and were thus in possession of the material resources for
experimentation and growth along nationalistic lines. Norway in
the middle years of the nineteenth century was in some respects
musically in a similar state to England at the same period: she had
her amateur choral societies, but no really efficient orchestra, and low
standards of performance in Christiania were among the reasons for
Grieg's unhappiness there. They may also be held to be the chief
cause of his failure to attain to complete mastery of the orchestral
medium, and of his reliance on the strings for many of his best
colour effects.

We have already seen that Grieg renounced symphonic writing
at an early stage in his career, yet continued for many years to make
repeated attempts to 'fight his way through the larger forms' and
to achieve some solution of the self-imposed problem of casting
genuine folk-material into the moulds of concerto and overture,
sonata and quartet. He failed repeatedly, as he was doomed to fail,
not only because folk-music obstinately refuses to become organically
part of a cyclic movement—witness the finale of Tchaikovsky's
Fourth Symphony, in which *The Birch Tree* seems in a fair way to

become a folk-tune to end all folk-tunes—but also because his grasp of structure was always his weakest point as a musician. Anyone could put his finger on the faults that every critic has taken pleasure in pointing to : the almost unbroken succession of two- and four-bar phrases, the mechanical repetitions and sequences which take away half the value of effects of colour by reiterating them until the hearer comes to detest them, the otiose note-for-note da capos, the blown-out climaxes leading to nothing in particular. Above all, there is the composer's inability to achieve rhythmic continuity throughout a sonata movement. He spreads his wings and soars aloft, returns to earth with a resounding thud, pauses, and begins all over again. Sometimes, indeed, he tried to make a virtue of necessity. Writing to a friend about his String Quartet in G minor[1] he says : ' You know that in my bigger works I have the habit, weakness, or call it what you will, of breaking off, for the sake of structural effect and thematic contrast, in the principal key before the second theme enters, instead of following the general practice of making a transition to lead imperceptibly into the latter. I do the same thing again after the return of the first subject in the recapitulation.'

Grieg had learned from Schumann and Chopin the use of contrapuntal devices both to enrich the texture and to join up the short sections so characteristic of romantic forms of expression. In dealing with folk-material Grieg developed such devices in many attractive ways, the more so as primitive canonic imitation is to be met with in folk-music itself. But in works of larger scope ingenuity is no substitute for breadth of conception; and that is why, for example, the first movement of the Piano Sonata—a movement that begins with high promise—fails so badly at the very point (near the beginning of the development section) where Grieg is being resourceful in chopping his principal theme into two halves which he proceeds to combine contrapuntally; in the meantime, the music stands still. With variation form Grieg was happier; it gave scope to his preference for writing short, well-contrasted, self-contained sections, each with its own rhythmic and harmonic colouring. The chief drawback common both to the Ballade for piano, Op. 24, and to the *Old Norwegian Melody* for two pianos, Op. 51, is that the themes are presented at the outset in too rich a setting; indeed, they are themselves too individual to be susceptible of the highest flights of the art of variation. The great masters of the form—Bach, Beethoven and Brahms—did not fall into this trap; in adopting themes for

---

[1] Letter to Frants Beyer, February 15, 1884.

variations they preferred those with the simplest outlines and studiously avoided those that contained some highly-coloured detail —such as the flattened third in the theme of Grieg's *Variations on an Old Norwegian Melody* (Ex. 98)—that would draw attention to itself and call for preferential treatment in each successive variation.

Although Grieg's short-breathed, square-cut phrases and mosaic-like methods of construction are partly the result of an innate lack of formal sense, partly a legacy from the early German romantics, they may also be looked upon in a more favourable light : as a definite though mild reaction against the Wagnerian despotism that cast its shadow over Western Europe during the last quarter of the nineteenth century. Grieg himself did not escape altogether from the all-pervading influence of *Tristan* and *The Ring*, but his recorded opinions on Wagner's treatment of the voice, on his ' endless melody ', and on the restlessness of his harmony leave no doubt of his antipathy to the prevailing tendencies of contemporary German music. Now the final liberation from Wagnerian and post-Wagnerian romanticism was to come from sources—notably the Russian Stravinsky and the Hungarian Bartók—in which anything like endless melody was eschewed in favour of brief, crisp, rhythmic motives springing directly from folk-music. Though a much slighter figure than either of the two modern composers just named, Grieg was in some ways their forerunner; a long-drawn melody, such as *Ingrid's Lament* (Prelude to Act II of *Peer Gynt*), is rarely met with in his works, whereas the reiterated semiquaver motive that opens the same prelude is so highly characteristic that we take it for granted in the light of later developments in European music.

Apart from Grieg's use of figures of this kind, derived in the main from folk-music and immediately attractive to his more unsophisticated contemporaries who were bored by the *longueurs* of Wagner and his followers, no one could claim that his music shows much rhythmic interest except in association with words. The exception is, however, more comprehensive than the rule, in that a very high proportion of his works have a literary basis, either directly as in the songs and dramatic music, or indirectly, as in the instrumental music based upon folk-themes. After the publication of the third Violin Sonata in 1887 Grieg completed no abstract instrumental work of any importance, although he made vain attempts to write a second String Quartet and a second Piano Concerto. His main artistic problem had in fact solved itself, though it left him frustrated and unhappy : the ' larger forms ' had been too much for him, and he had

had to reconcile himself to follow what we now recognise as his true vocation : that of a miniaturist, a mood-painter, a recorder of fleeting impressions. Henceforth he was to employ his talents as a creative artist in the mating of words (chiefly in a beautiful but hitherto little regarded tongue) with music that enhanced their natural rhythm and cadence; in exploring new and rich sonorities of choral voices, of the pianoforte, and of bowed strings; and above all in the enrichment of his style by novel and striking colourings. As he resigned himself to his failure to blend the national ideals he fervently admired with the traditions of composition he respected, he allowed himself to be drawn ever more closely to the vigorous and dignified culture of the Norwegian peasantry. As the years went by he absorbed more and more of what they had to teach him, and in doing so he strengthened his own originality. The finest of his achievements are therefore those in which he accepts thankfully the gifts of the Norwegian countryside and its peoples and reverently, without concessions to polite society such as he had been willing to make in his earlier days, gave them to the world with the imprint of his own personality. It is these works that the world knows and understands least : the Vinje and *Haugtussa* songs, the part-songs for male voices, the *Slåtter* for piano, and the choral Psalms.

It would scarcely be possible, even if it were useful, to separate in Grieg's musical language its several constituents of melody, harmony and texture, so inextricably are they interwoven. One of its most salient features, for example, is the use of melodic figures drawn out of chords of the seventh and ninth, as in the Prelude to Act I of *Peer Gynt* (Ex. 92). Similar passages occur in Solveig's lullaby in the last Act of the same work (at the words ' Gutten har hvilet ved sin moders bryst '), in the *Bridal Procession* for piano (*Pictures of Folk Life*) and in many other places.

The use of melodic formulae of this kind, derived from single chords, is of the greatest help in maintaining the tranquillity of harmonic background after which Grieg so often strives. I have already mentioned his dislike of Wagner's later style in several particulars; and there is an instructive passage in one of his critical notes on *The Ring*, written from Bayreuth in 1876, in which he comments on the lack of ' points of repose ' in Wagner's music and refers to ' the numerous chromatic transitions, the ceaseless changes of harmony, which result in one's being gradually overcome by nervous irritability, and finally by complete apathy '. Words like these may sound strange coming from a composer in whose own idiom chromaticism plays so important a part; but, as we shall see presently, Wagner and Grieg use this resource in very different ways. In the meantime, it is enough to note the static quality of much of Grieg's harmony, whether chromatic or diatonic.[1] Some of his happiest effects are achieved by the most economical use of the simplest chords, carefully disposed, as in the charming opening of the third *Haugtussa* song (Ex. 93).

Like his Russian contemporaries, Grieg often obtains a modal or quasi-modal colouring by means of diatonic triads in root position; but such a passage as Ex. 94 from the song *Udfarten*, quite an early work, has a distinction all its own and could hardly have been written by any other composer; the acciaccature in the piano part are strangely affecting, and so are the slightly jarring A's and B's in the penultimate bar.

Grieg's addiction to modal melody and harmony is of course a natural corollary of his use of folk-material. In his earlier settings of folk-tune he is often somewhat diffident in his handling of modal passages, rounding off the whole with a cadence in the conventional major or minor. Later he abandoned such compromises, and even went out of the way to set up modal associations, particularly around the fifth degree of the normal major or minor scale. A good example of such an effect of 'mixolydian' tonality occurs in the same song, *Udfarten* (Ex. 95). But there are other and even more interesting references, direct or oblique, to the scales of folk-music. Thus one of Grieg's favourite chords, that of the added sixth, acquires special associations from being made up of the notes of the goathorn, as in the first bars of *Kulok* (*Norwegian Folk-Tunes*, Op. 66, No. 1) (Ex. 96).

Then the stringed instruments of the Norwegian dales, the langleik and the Hardanger fiddle with its sympathetic strings, help to explain a number of unusual and fascinating progressions. Gerald Abraham has shown, in his study of *Chopin's Musical Style*,[2] how important a part the sharpened fourth, common in Polish folk-music, plays not only in colouring Chopin's melodies, but also in forming some of his most striking harmonic combinations. Norwegian music too possesses this sharpened fourth, and an examination of Grieg's *Slåtter* shows how skilfully he turned it to account, treating it at one moment as an essential melody note, at another as a diatonic passing

---

[1] Fischer's exhaustive study of Grieg's harmonic style has already been mentioned by Mrs. Dale.

[2] Oxford University Press, 1939.

note on dominant harmony, at another as an element in the construction of striking dissonances, or again as the starting-point for one
of his characteristic chromatic progressions of the bass or a middle
part (cf. Exs. 60, 61 and 97*a* and *b*). Nor is the fourth of the scale
the only inflected note appearing in Norwegian folk-music. In his
work on Hungarian folk-song Bela Bartók[1] remarks that the third
of the Hungarian scale is variable, and that the ' natural ' and ' flat '
variants may even appear in the same melody. Norwegian folk-
music also has these interchangeable thirds, and Grieg takes advantage of them (as Kjerulf had done before him) in harmonising the
ballad tune (Ex. 98) on which his *Old Norwegian Melody* for two
pianos, Op. 51, is based.

One of the secrets of the charm of Grieg's music at its best is due
to such half-naïve, half-sophisticated procedures, whereby a chord or
progression takes on a double meaning : either as a touch of colour
taken from the current harmonic vocabulary of the later Romantic
period, or as a stylised derivation from one of the features of folk-
music. Such, for example, is the twofold character of the well-known
bars quoted as Ex. 99, from the song *Våren* (equally well known
as one of the *Elegiac Melodies* for strings, under the title *The Last
Spring*). The melody here is easily explained as being based on the
ascending forms of the melodic minor scale of classical usage, with
a chromatic triad in the harmony at the cadence-point; and yet one
feels in one's bones that it is something quite different. The suggestion is rather of a derivative from a scale neither minor nor modal,
but peculiar to the folk-tune of a particular region. Similarly, a
composition like the *Lualåt* (Mountaineer's Song), Op. 73, No. 7,
while having the appearance on paper of an exercise in late nineteenth-century chromaticism, is in reality based on the folk-scale with
its sharpened fourth and variable third. It is instructive to place an
excerpt from this piece side by side with part of the cor anglais solo
from the opening of the Third Act of Wagner's *Tristan* (Ex. 100).
Approximately the same picturesque effect is intended by both composers—the sound of a pastoral pipe in desolate mountain country :
but whereas Grieg keeps very closely within the limits of the peculiar
folk-scale he has chosen to imitate, Wagner produces a feeling of
intense restlessness by deliberately obscuring all semblance of tonality
during the passage quoted. In this case his emotional aim is of course
entirely different from Grieg's; but on the whole the passage is typical

[1] *A Magyar Népdal* (Budapest, 1924); English version, *Hungarian Folk Music*
(Oxford University Press, 1931).

of Wagner's use of the chromatic scale in his mature style, and we already know how Grieg reacted to that style. Even when employing the normal chromatic scale quite freely for decorative or colouristic purposes Grieg usually takes measures to counteract a good deal of its natural restlessness. One of these measures is to keep the melody strictly diatonic while the bass or inner parts glide about in semitones. There are plenty of examples of this procedure, one very typical case occurring in the *Bondens Sang* (Peasant's Song), Op. 65, No. 2, another at the close of Solveig's lullaby. Another means of resisting the pull of the chromatic scale against the tonic and thereby ensuring comparative tranquillity in the harmonic scheme is one that plays so important a part in Grieg's technical equipment that it deserves separate consideration.

Drone basses, forming what our harmony text-books call pedal-points, direct or inverted, are a rudimentary form of polyphony common to almost all primitive music from China to Peru. One proof of its ubiquity in Europe at least is the wide distribution of instruments, particularly those of the bagpipe family, that are equipped to sound one or more notes as a perpetual accompaniment whatever melodies are played on the chanter. Medieval Norway, and certain closely associated areas such as Iceland and the Faroes, evolved more than one stringed instrument similarly equipped. The Hardanger fiddle has already been mentioned; not only does it possess a set of sympathetic strings beneath the fingerboard whose purpose is to enrich the tone of the bowed strings with an ethereal quality which, according to Halvorsen, can only be faintly imitated on the ordinary violin by the use of the mute, but it can be tuned in several ways, all tending to facilitate an accompaniment of drones and also of stationary or moving fourths, fifths and occasionally other intervals to melodies played on it. Then there was the langleik, now almost obsolete, a plucked instrument one of whose eight strings may be tuned, according to one system, to G and carries the melody while the remaining seven vibrate freely to the notes C, c^1, g^1, c^2, d^2, e^2, g^2. The correspondences between these sounds and the harmonic series can hardly be accidental, and point to the real purpose of the ' drone chord '—to increase the resonance of the melody string and colour the tone of the instrument in the same way that results from the depression of the damper pedal of the pianoforte. Now it is not suggested that Grieg needed to study folk-music in order to discover the pedal-point, any more than folk-music was the direct cause of his interest in unusual chords and chromatic progressions. Pedal-points have been part of the stock-in-trade of composers at every period of which we have substantial knowledge. What is certain, however, is that as with the use of the chromatic scale, or the mixture of duplet and triplet quaver groupings, Grieg's enthusiasm for folk-music disposed him to exploit various pedal devices, to introduce them more and more often into his arrangements and original works, and to employ them in novel ways. An interesting example of cross-fertilisation between a convention from the main tradition of European music and a folk-idiom occurs in the first Violin Sonata, Op. 8, whose allegretto quasi andantino, though obviously representing the customary minuet, partakes strongly of the character of the Norwegian springdans; and the trio (più vivo) falls naturally into line with the classical musette (again a dance of folk origin, employing, as its name indicates, a 'bagpipe' bass) while imitating the double-string playing associated with the Hardanger fiddle.

But this by no means exhausts the function of pedal-notes in Grieg's musical vocabulary. We have seen that chromaticism in Grieg does not by any means always make for restlessness; on the contrary, he often produces a remarkably tranquil effect by combining a smooth, diatonic melody, or one based on a modal or folk-scale with a semitonal inner part. In a great many cases when this occurs we find another quiescent element in the texture : a pedal-point that by its inertia counteracts the fluid chromatic part, which thereby tends to become nothing more nor less than a vividly-coloured strand in the harmonic fabric. An example of this procedure has already been given (Ex. 100a); scores of others may be found in Grieg's works, such as Nos. 3 and 12 of the Vinje Songs, Op. 33, *Den Sårede* and *Fyremål*, in the closing bars of Solveig's lullaby, in the *Norwegian Dances*, Op. 35, in the *Folk Tunes*, Op. 66, and above all in the *Slåtter*, Op. 72.

In this last-named work Grieg reaches so far into the future that very few music-lovers—much less professional pianists—have even now caught up with him, and these remarkable pieces remain unplayed except in Norway itself, where they have had a considerable influence on contemporary composers. Here we meet with more than one hint of a trend of development that music was to follow in the next quarter of a century : the combination of tonalities. Even in a very minor work, the Valse-Impromptu from the *Lyric Pieces* (Op. 47, No. 1), the opening bars (Ex. 101) break fresh ground with a tonal ambiguity that makes any attempt at theoretic explanation on orthodox lines sound like special pleading. It is all very well to say that we have here a somewhat wilful start on subdominant harmony proceeding on its lawful occasions below a somewhat wayward melody in the melodic minor (ascending form used both ways—or call it a folk-scale if we will). But that is not what the passage sounds like. The aural effect is, during the first four or five bars at least, that of a left-hand part in A minor and a right-hand part in E major. The suggestion of bitonality is much stronger than in the passage (Ex. 102) in the Four Psalms, Op. 74, mentioned by Mr. Rubbra,[1] where a complex notation disguises a comparatively simple progression based on the mixolydian mode.

Grieg's treatment of dissonant harmonies is often bold and, again, even prophetic. His diatonic sevenths, ninths, and elevenths are still so fresh to him as masses of sonority, apart from their meaning in the context, that he is often tempted to dwell on them with naïve delight, as in the familiar *Bridal Procession*, Op. 19, No. 2, or in the Piano Concerto, thereby weakening the structure of his music, and also drawing attention to his habit of composing at the keyboard. The same improvisational character belongs to such impressionistic passages as Ex. 103 from *Skovstilhed* (Peace of the Woods), Op. 71, No. 4, with its deferred resolutions and parallel chord movement that would hardly sound out of place in a Debussy prelude. The remarkable little piece *Klokkeklang* (Bell-Ringing), Op. 54, No. 6, is even more advanced; with its superimposed, jarring open fifths it carries us right outside the classical and romantic system of harmony into regions where entirely different conceptions of chord structure and syntax hold sway. Many of Grieg's progressions obstinately refuse to be explained on theoretical grounds; beginning quite innocently, they take a sudden turn that places them beyond discussion in terms of tonic, dominant, pedal-points and so forth. Such a passage is Ex. 104 from *Fiskervise*, one of the *Seven Children's Songs*, Op. 61.

One might indeed state, as a fundamental principle of Grieg's mature harmonic style, his determination to get away from the traditional relationships of tonic and dominant; and it is worth analysing some of the stratagems he employs to avoid or disguise the formula V–I. One favourite device is to invert the dominant triad or seventh or substitute for it the *augmented* triad, whose meaning is more equivocal than that of the more usual chords; another is to create the illusion of static harmony by the use of pedal-points, as already described; another is to quit a dominant harmony,

[1] See p. 109.

once it has been reached, by treating it as a chromatic chord in relation to what follows. *Til Foråret* (To the Spring), Op. 43, No. 6, provides a compendium of such devices; sugary though it may sound to us after sixty years of harmonic revolution, it must have been exciting enough in its day to influence more than one school of young composers. Sibelius in particular often seems to give back echoes of Grieg, not only in melodic and harmonic tendencies, such as the use of augmented triads, but also in certain tricks of lay-out, such as doubling the melody an octave below an accompaniment of sustained or reiterated chords. From this point of view, comparison of *The Swan of Tuonela* with the Grieg piano piece just referred to is not without interest.

The world of music owes a debt to the minority of executants, critics and amateurs who make it their business to call our attention from time to time to the claims of the *petits maîtres*, inciting us to enquire not only into the defects that kept them *petits* but also into the virtues that made them *maîtres*. The only qualification that should be required of a creative artist is that we should, on his behalf, be able to give a positive answer to Schubert's habitual question : ' *Kann er was?* ' Can he do anything? In other words, is he a personality in the musical sense? Whether he is a great artist or a small one is another question. We cannot always be surrounded by Schuberts. This chapter has been written as an attempt to show that Grieg, one of the most curiously inhibited and circumscribed composers ever to obtain wide recognition, not only had something significant to say, but said it in an idiom quite unmistakably his own. A devoted son of a small nation renowned for its courage, originality and independence of spirit, he succeeded in striking out a path in another direction from the crowded, somewhat dusty highroad of German late romanticism. The path was undoubtedly a narrow one, and many will say that it led nowhere. But the adventure was bravely conceived, and at least resulted in discoveries that we may well be grateful for : unsuspected treasures of poetry among rocks and forests, rich and delightful sonorities heard in the loneliness of unfrequented places, a lifting of the heart at the touch of a fresh and childlike imagination.

Chronology

1843.   Born, June 15, at Bergen.

About 1855. First essay in composition.

1858–62. At Leipzig Conservatoire.

1860.   Serious illness (pleurisy).

1862.   First concert in Bergen.

1863–6. Lives mostly in Copenhagen.

1864.   Symphony in C minor; betrothal to Nina Hagerup.

1864–6. Friendship with Nordraak.

1865.   Piano Sonata and first Violin Sonata; first visit to Italy (December to following summer).

1866.   *Autumn* Overture; settles in Christiania (October).

1867.   Conducts Christiania Harmonic Society; marriage (June 11); second Violin Sonata; first book of *Lyric Pieces*.

1868.   Birth of daughter, Alexandra (April 10); Piano Concerto.

1869.   Death of Alexandra; discovery of Lindeman's collection of Norwegian folk-music.

1869–70. Second visit to Rome; meeting with Liszt.

1871.   Foundation of the Christiania Musikforening.

1872.   *Sigurd Jorsalfar* produced.

1874.   Granted Government pension; move to Bergen; *Peer Gynt* music begun.

1875.   Death of parents; Ballade in G minor.

1876.   *Peer Gynt* produced; hears *Ring* at Bayreuth.

1876–89. Estrangement from Björnson.

1877.   Move to Hardanger.

1877–8. G minor Quartet; *Den Bergtekne*; *Album for Male Voices*.

1880.   Vinje songs (Op. 33).

1880–2. Conducts Bergen Harmonien.

1883.   'Cello Sonata.

1883–4. Concert tour in Germany, Holland and Italy.

1884.   *Holberg* Suite.

1885.   Move to new house (Troldhaugen).

1887.   C minor Violin Sonata.

1888.   First visit to England.

1889.   First visit to Paris.

1895.   *Haugtussa* songs.

1898.   Festival of Norwegian Music at Bergen; *Symphonic Dances*.

1899.   Dreyfus letter.

I

1900.   Serious deterioration of health; last songs.

1901.   Last book of *Lyric Pieces*.

1902–3.   *Slåtter*.

1903.   Anti-Dreyfusard demonstration in Paris; sixtieth birthday
          celebrations.

1905.   Separation of Norwegian and Swedish crowns.

1906.   Meeting with Percy Grainger.

1907.   Dies, September 4.

Bibliography

As in the other volumes of this series, the bibliography is selective rather than exhaustive. It includes books and articles dealing with the music rather than with the man, though primary biographical sources, including important correspondence, are given.—ED.

CALVOCORESSI, M. D.: 'An unpublished letter of Grieg's' (in *Monthly Musical Record*, January 1932).

CAPELLEN, GEORG: *Die Freiheit oder Unfreiheit der Töne und Intervalle als Kriterium der Stimmführung nebst einem Anhang*: *Grieg-Analysen als Bestätigungsnachweis und Wegweiser der neuen Musiktheorie* (Leipzig, 1904).

CLOSSEN, E.: *Edvard Grieg et la musique scandinave* (offprint from *Guide musical*, Brussels) (Paris, 1892).

DALE, KATHLEEN: 'Edvard Grieg's Pianoforte Music' (in *Music and Letters*, October 1943).

DESMOND, ASTRA: 'Grieg's Songs' (in *Music and Letters*, October 1941).

FELLERER, K. G.: *Edvard Grieg* (Potsdam, 1942).

FINCK, H. T.: *Edvard Grieg* (John Lane, London, 1906; second edition, much enlarged, 1929).

FISCHER, KURT VON: *Griegs Harmonik und die nordländische Folklore* (Bern and Leipzig, 1938).

FOERSTER, J. B.: *Edvard Hagerup Grieg* (Prague, 1890).

GILMAN, LAWRENCE: Chapter on Grieg in *Phases of Modern Music* (John Lane, London, and Harper, New York, 1904).

GRAINGER, PERCY: 'Personal Recollections of Grieg' (in *Musical Times*, XLVIII, No. 777).

GRIEG, EDVARD: 'My First Success' (in *Contemporary Review*, London, July 1905).

    Breve fra Grieg (Copenhagen, 1922).

    Breve fra Edvard Grieg til Frants Beyer, 1872–1907 (Christiania, 1923).

    Briefe an die Verleger der Edition Peters, 1866–1907 (Leipzig, 1932).

    Et Festskrift i Anledning af Griegs 60-Årige Födselsdag (Bergen, 1903).

HORTON, JOHN: 'Grieg's "Slåtter" for Pianoforte' (in *Music and Letters*, October 1945).

    'Ibsen, Grieg and *Peer Gynt*' (in *Music and Letters*, April 1945).

KRETZSCHMAR, HERMANN: Kritik von Griegs Op. 23, 27–9, 31, 32, 35–8 (in *Musikalisches Wochenblatt*, Leipzig, 1884, No. 42–3).

'Grieg's Lyrische Stücke: eine Würdigung' (Preface to Peters' collected edition) (Leipzig, 1902).

Griegs Klavierkonzert (Breitkopfs Konzertführer, No. 598) (Leipzig, N.D.).

Griegs Suiten, Op. 46 und 55 (Breitkopfs Konzertführer, No. 560) Leipzig, N.D.).

KÜHN, A.: 'Richard Wagner's Vermächtnis' (on Grieg's *Olaf Trygvason*) (in *Schweizerische Musikzeitung*, Vol. XXXIV, Nos. 18–19).

KWAST, JAMES: *Griegs Klavierkonzert* (Schlesinger's Musikführer, No. 70) (Berlin, N.D.).

LA MARA: 'Edvard Grieg' (in *Peters' Grieg Catalogue*, Leipzig, 1898). Chapter on Grieg in *Musikalische Studienköpfe*, Vol. III (Leipzig, 1910).

MASON, D. G.: Chapter on Grieg in *From Grieg to Brahms* (New York, 1902; reissue by Macmillan, New York, 1904).

MONRAD-JOHANSEN, D.: *Edvard Grieg* (Oslo, 1934; English translation by Madge Robertson, Princeton University Press, 1938).

MUZALEVSKY, V.: *Edvard Grieg* (Leningrad, 1935).

NIEMANN, WALTER: *Die Musik Skandinaviens* (Leipzig, 1906).

Die nordische Klaviermusik (Leipzig, 1917).

(See also under Schjelderup.)

PLATZHOFF-LEJEUNE, E.: 'Aus Briefen Edvard Griegs an einen Schweizer' (in *Die Musik*, Jahrgang VII, No. 2).

ROKSETH, YVONNE: *Grieg* (Paris, 1933).

RÖNTGEN, JULIUS: *Grieg* (mainly Grieg's letters to Röntgen) (s'Gravenhage, 1930).

'Edvard Griegs musikalischer Nachlass' (in *Die Musik*, Jahrgang VII, No. 5).

SANDVIK, O. M.: 'E. Grieg und die norwegische Volksmusik' (in *Gedenboeck aangeboden aan Dr. D. F. Scheurleer*) (s'Gravenhage, 1925). (See also under Schjelderup)

SCHJELDERUP, GERHARD: *Edvard Grieg og hans Værker.* (Copenhagen, 1903.)

'Edvard Grieg als Klavierkomponist' (in *Der Kunstwart*, Munich, XVIII, No. 2).

'Über Griegs Violinsonaten' (in *Neue Musikzeitung*, Stuttgart, XXV, No. 21).

SCHJELDERUP and NIEMANN: *Edvard Grieg: Biographie und Würdigung seiner Werke* (Leipzig, 1908).

SCHJELDERUP and SANDVIK: *Norges Musikhistorie* (Oslo, 1921).

SCHMID, OTTO: 'Edvard Grieg' (in *Neue Zeitschrift für Musik*, LXIV, Nos. 26–30).

STEIN, RICHARD: *Grieg* (Berlin, 1921).

DE STOECKLIN, PAUL: *Grieg* (Paris, 1926).

VOROSHILOV, H.: *Edvard Grieg* (St. Petersburg, 1898).

VAN WESTRHENE, P. A.: *Edvard Grieg* (Haarlem, 1897).

Chronological List of Compositions

(with page references)

Grieg's numerous arrangements of his own music are generally given under the original form of the work; transcriptions and excerpts are entered separately only when the composer gave them different opus numbers and in one or two cases where the transcribed form is more familiar than the original. 'Arranged' means ' arranged by the composer '; the innumerable arrangements by other musicians are ignored.

ORCHESTRAL WORKS

Opus No.

None. Symphony in C minor (1864; see under Piano Duets).

11. Concert overture, *I Höst* (In Autumn) (1866; arranged for piano duet and published as *Fantasie*, 1867; reorchestrated 1887, at first as *Concert Overture* without title): 17–20, 23, 26, 77, 113.

16. Concerto in A minor for piano and orchestra (1868; drastically revised 1906–7): 7, 16, 20–1, 22–4, 26–34, 37, 40, 42, 44–5, 49, 53, 58, 67–8, 126.

46. First Suite from the music to *Peer Gynt*, Op. 23 (four numbers— *Morning Mood, The Death of Aase, Anitra's Dance* and *In the Hall of the Dovre-King*—revised and reorchestrated 1888) (arranged for piano solo and piano duet) (see under Dramatic Works).

51. *Old Norwegian Melody with Variations* (see Works for Two Pianos).

55. Second Suite from the music to *Peer Gynt*, Op. 23 (four numbers— *The Abduction and Ingrid's Lament, Arabian Dance, Peer Gynt's Homecoming* and *Solveig's Song*[1]—revised and reorchestrated 1891) (arranged for piano solo and piano duet) (see under Dramatic Works).

56. Three Orchestral Pieces from the music to *Sigurd Jorsalfar*, Op. 22 (*Prelude*: *In the King's Hall*, based on Op. 22, No. 2—see also under Chamber Music; *Intermezzo*: *Borghild's Dream*, based on Op. 22, No. 1; *Homage March*, expanded from Op. 22, No. 4, with introductory fanfare, trio, etc, added; revised and reorchestrated 1892) (arranged for piano solo and piano duet) (see under Dramatic Works).

[1] It appears from Grieg's letter to Röntgen of February 19, 1893, that the Second Suite originally included one more number, the Dovre-King's daughter's dance, Op. 23, No. 8.

Opus No.

64. Symphonic Dances (1898) (also for piano duet)[1]: 17, 21–4, 27, 41, 64. Sketches for second Piano Concerto in B minor (1883): 28, 120.

WORKS FOR STRING ORCHESTRA

34. Two Elegiac Melodies: No. 1, *Herzwunden* (The Wounded Heart); No. 2, *Letzter Frühling* (The Last Spring), based on the songs Op. 33, I, Nos. 3 and 2 (1881) (arranged for piano solo and piano duet): 17, 22, 123.

40. Suite, *Fra Holbergs Tid* (From Holberg's Time) (see under Works for Piano Solo).

53. Two Melodies: No. 1, *Norsk* (Norwegian); No. 2, *Det Förste Möde* (First Meeting), based on the songs, Op. 33, II, No. 6 and Op. 21, No. 1 (1891) (arranged for piano solo): 17, 22, 88.

63 Two Norwegian Melodies: No. 1, *In Folk Style*, based on a melody by Fr. Due; No. 2, *Cow-call and Peasant Dance*, based on the folk-tunes *So lokka me over den myra* and *Stabbe-Låtten*; cf. Works for Piano Solo, Op. 17, Nos. 22 and 18 (1895) (arranged for piano solo and piano duet): 17, 22, 24, 64.

68, No. 5. *Bådnlåt* (At the Cradle) (cf. Works for Piano Solo).

CHAMBER MUSIC

None. String Quartet (lost) (1861).

8. Sonata No. 1, in F, for violin and piano (1865): 26, 32, 35, 40–1, 63, 67, 125.

None. Gavotte for violin and piano (1867; orchestrated 1872, as Op. 22, No. 2; revised 1892, as Op. 56, No. 1: see *Sigurd Jorsalfar*, under Dramatic Works and Orchestral Works).

13. Sonata No. 2, in G, for violin and piano (1867): 26, 32, 35, 38–9, 68.

27. String Quartet in G minor (based largely on the song *Spillemaend*, Op. 25, No. 1) (1877–8): 8, 28, 32, 34, 41–3, 82, 112, 119.

None. Andante in C minor, for piano, violin and 'cello (1878): 44.

36. Sonata in A minor, for 'cello and piano (1883): 32–3, 35–6, 40–1, 67.

45. Sonata No. 3, in C minor, for violin and piano (1887): 32–3, 35–40, 67–8, 113, 120.

None. First two movements of a String Quartet in F (1891): 32, 41–4, 120. Sketches for a Piano Quintet in B flat (1886?): 44.

WORKS FOR PIANO SOLO

'1' Variations on a German Melody (about 1855).

None. Fugue on GADE (about 1860).

---

[1] I have been unable to determine which was the original form of Op. 64: orchestral or piano duet. The thematic material of No. 1 is a halling from Valders, of No. 2 another halling, of No. 3 a springdans from Aamot; No. 4 is based on the song *Saag du nokke kjaeringa mi* and a wedding tune from Valders (cf. Works for Piano Solo, Op. 17, Nos. 23 and 24).

Opus No.

1.   *Fire Klaver Stykker* (Four Piano Pieces) (1862). No. 1, Allegro con leggerezza (D major); 2, Non allegro e molto espress. (C major); 3, Mazurka (A minor); 4, Allegro con moto (E minor): 47–8.

3.   *Poetiske Tonebilleder* (Six Poetic Tone-Pictures) (1863). No. 1, Allegro ma non troppo (E minor); 2, Allegro cantabile (B flat); 3, Con moto (C minor); 4, Andante con sentimento (A major); 5, Allegro moderato (F major); 6, Allegro scherzando (E minor): 46, 48, 114.

28, No. 1. *Albumblad* (Album-leaf) in A flat (1864): 46–50.

None. *Sörgemarsj over Rikard Nordraak* (Funeral March in A minor for Rikard Nordraak) (1866, transposed to G minor and arranged for military band, 1867): 116.

6.   *Humoresker* (1865): 46, 48–9, 63, 67, 114.

7.   Sonata in E minor (1865): 21, 26, 32, 40, 45, 57–8, 67, 115.

12.   *Lyriske Stykker* (Lyric Pieces) I (1867): No. 1, *Arietta*; 2, *Vals* (Waltz); 3, *Vægtersang* (Watchman's Song); 4, *Alfedans* (Fairy Dance); 5, *Folkevise* (Folksong); 6, *Norsk* (Norwegian Melody); 7, *Albumblad* (Album Leaf); 8, *Fædrelandssang* (National Song) (arranged for voices with words by Björnson) (1868): 49, 51–2, 115.

17   *Norske danser og viser* (Norwegian Dances and Songs) (1870). No. 1, Springdans (from Gol in Hallingdal; 2, *Ungersvenden han bad sin pige* (The young man asked his maiden) (from Vaage); 3, Springdans; 4, *Niels Tallefjorn den kaute karen* (Niels Tallefjorn, proud fellow); 5, Jölstring (Dance from Jölster); 6, Brulaat (Bridal March) (from Gol in Hallingdal); 7, Halling (from Osterdal); 8, *Aa grisen hadde eit tryne* (Oh, the pig had a snout) (from Hjertdal); 9, *Naar mit öie* (When my tired eyes) (religious song from Hitterdal); 10, *Aa Ole engang i sinde* (Ole once in anger); 11, *På Dovrefjeld i Norge* (On the Dovrefjeld in Norway) (from Haukelie); 12, *Solfager og Ormekongen* (Solfager and the Snake-King) (from Mo in Telemark); 13, *Reiselåt* (march for the bridal procession when it leaves the church) (from Gol in Hallingdal); 14, *Jeg sjunger med et sorrigfuldt hjerte* (I sing with a sorrowful heart) (from Valders); 15, *Den sidste laurdags kvelden* (The last Saturday night); 16, *Je veit ei lita jente* (I know a little maiden); 17, *Aa kleggen han sa no te flugga si* (The gadfly said to the fly); 18, *Stabbe-Låtten* (comic 'stumping' dance from Valders) (cf. Works for String Orchestra, Op. 63, No. 2); 19, *Hölje Dale* (from Sillegjord); 20, Halling; 21, *Sae bygga*; 22, *So lokka me over den myra* (cow-calling song from Valders) (cf. Works for String Orchestra, Op. 63, No. 2); 23, *Saag du nokke kjaeringa mi* (cf. Symphonic Dance, Op. 64, No. 4); 24, *Brulåt* (bridal song from Valders) (cf. Symphonic Dance, Op. 64, No. 4); 25, *Ravna Bryllupet i Kraakalund* (The Ravens' Wedding) (from Sogn): 26, 62–4, 67, 69.

OPUS NO.

19.   *Folkelivsbilleder* (Scenes from Folk-Life) (1872): 1, *Fjeldslåt* (On
the Mountains); 2, *Brudefölget drar forbi* (The Bridal Procession
passes by) (arranged for piano duet; Halvorsen's orchestration
included in *Peer Gynt* music, as Op. 23, No. 2); 3, *Fra
Karnevalet* (Carnival Scene): 46, 55, 61, 66–7, 69, 104, 121, 126.

28, No. 2. *Albumblad* (Album-leaf) in F (1874): 46, 50.

24.   *Ballade i form av variasjoner over en norsk folkevise* (Ballade in
the form of variations on a Norwegian folk-song) (Based on
Den Nordlandske bondestand, The Nordland Yeoman, from
Valders) (1875): 21, 27, 45, 47, 49, 58–61, 65, 119.

None. *Seks norske Fjeldmelodier* (Six Norwegian Mountain-Melodies)
(not later than 1875): 1, *Springdans* (from Nummedal);
2, *Bådn-Låt* (Lullaby) (from Valders); 3, *Springdans* (from
Vinje); 4, *Sjugur å Trollbrura* (Sigurd and the Troll-Bride) (cf.
Works for Two Pianos, Op. 51); 5, Halling (from Österdalen);
6, *Guten å gjenta på fjöshjellen* (The boy and girl in the cow-
barn) (cf. Op. 29, No. 1 below): 61–2, 64.

28, Nos. 3 and 4. *Albumblade* (Album-leaves) in A major (1876) and
C sharp minor (1878): 44, 46, 50.

29.   *Improvisata over norske folkeviser* (Improvisata on Norwegian
folk-tunes) (1878): No. 1, *Guten å gjenta på fjöshjellen* (The boy
and girl in the cow-barn) (cf. *Seks norske Fjeldmelodier* above);
2, *Dae va eigong en Kungje* (There was once a king) (from
Valders): 61–2.

38.   *Lyriske Stykker* (Lyric Pieces) II (1883): 1, *Vuggevise* (Berceuse);
2, *Folkevise* (Folk-song); 3, *Melodie*; 4, Halling[1]; 5, *Springdans*;
6, *Elegie*; 7, *Vals* (Waltz); 8, *Kanon*: 48, 54, 67, 115.

40.   Suite, *Fra Holbergs Tid* (From Holberg's Time) (1884: arranged
for string orchestra, 1885): No. 1, Prelude; 2, Sarabande;
3, Gavotte; 4, Air; 5, Rigaudon: 17, 21–2, 24–5, 35, 46, 48,
50, 116.

41.   Song Transcriptions (1885): 1, *Vuggesang* (Cradle Song) (Op. 9,
No. 2); 2, *Liden Håkon* (Little Haakon) (Op. 15, No. 1); 3, *Jeg
elsker dig* (I love thee) (Op. 5, No. 3); 4, *Hun er saa hvid* (She is
so white) (Op. 18, No. 2); 5, *Prinsessen* (The Princess) (no opus
number); 6, *Jeg giver mit digt til våren* (I give my song to the
Spring) (Op. 21, No. 3).

43.   *Lyriske Stykker* (Lyric Pieces) III (1886): 1, *Sommerfugl*
(Butterfly); 2, *Ensom Vandrer* (Lonely Wanderer); 3, *I
Hjemmet* (In my Native Country); 4, *Liden Fugl* (Little Bird);
5, *Erotik*; 6, *Til Foråret* (To the Spring): 48, 52, 56, 67, 127.

47.   *Lyriske Stykker* (Lyric Pieces) IV (1888): 1, *Valse-Impromptu*;
2, *Albumblad* (Album Leaf); 3, *Melodie*; 4, Halling (arranged
from the *Peer Gynt* music, Op. 23, No. 3); 5, *Melankoli*;
6, *Springdans*; 7, *Elegie*: 54–6, 66–7, 125.

[1] The strain beginning at bar 9 is taken from the folk-song *Paal paa hougje* (Paul
on the hill).

Opus No.

52. Song Transcriptions (1891): 1, *Modersorg* (A Mother's grief) (Op. 15, No. 4); 2, *Det förste Möde* (The first Meeting) (Op. 21, No. 1); 3, *Du fatter ej Bölgernes evige Gang* (You know not the waves' eternal motion) (Op. 5, No. 2); 4, *Solveigs Sang* (from *Peer Gynt*); 5, *Kjærlighed* (Love) (Op. 15, No. 2); 6, *Gamle Mor* (Old Mother) (Op. 33, II, No. 1).

None. *Hvide Skyer* (Tempest Clouds) (unfinished; completed by Röntgen) (1891): 57.

54. *Lyriske Stykker* (Lyric Pieces) V (1891)[1]: 1, *Gjætergut* (Shepherd Boy); 2, *Gangar* (Norwegian March); 3, *Troldtog* (March of the Dwarfs); 4, *Notturno*; 5, *Scherzo*; 6, *Klokkeklang* (Bell-Ringing): 17, 52, 66–9, 126.

57. *Lyriske Stykker* (Lyric Pieces) VI (1893): 1, *Svundne Dage* (Vanished Days); 2, *Gade*; 3, *Illusion*; 4, *Hemmelighed* (Secret); 5, *Hun danser* (She dances); 6, *Hjemve* (Home-Sickness): 50, 52, 54, 65, 67–8.

62. *Lyriske Stykker* (Lyric Pieces) VII (1895): 1, *Sylphe*; 2, *Tak* (Gratitude); 3, *Fransk Serenade* (French Serenade); 4, *Bækken* (The Brook); 5, *Drömmesyn* (Phantom); 6, *Hjemad* (Homeward): 52–4, 68.

65. *Lyriske Stykker* (Lyric Pieces) VIII (1896): 1, *Fra Ungdomsdagene* (From Early Years); 2, *Bondens Sang* (Peasant's Song); 3, *Tungsind* (Melancholy); 4, *Salon*; 5, *I Balladetone* (In Ballad Vein); 6, *Bryllupsdag på Troldhaugen* (Wedding-Day at Troldhaugen): 54–6, 124.

66. *Norske Folkeviser* (Norwegian Folk-Tunes) (1896): No. 1, *Kulok* (Cow-call) (from Lom); 2, *Det er den störste Dårlighed* (It is the greatest folly) (from Söndmöre)[2]; 3, *En Konge hersked i Österland* (A king ruled in the East) (from Sogn); 4, *Siri Dale Visen* (The Siri Dale Song) (from Aardal, Sogn); 5, *Det var i min Ungdom* ('Twas in my youth) (from Lyster, Sogn); 6, *Lok og Bådnlåt* (Call and Lullaby) (from Lyster); 7, *Bådnlåt* (Lullaby) (from Ryfylke); 8, *Lok* (Call) (from Lom); 9, *Liten va Guten* (It was a little fellow) (from Östre Slidre); 10, *Morgo ska du få gifte deg* (To-morrow you shall marry) (from Lom); 11, *Der stander to Piger* (There stood two girls) (from Lom); 12, *Ranveig* (from Lom); 13, *En liten grå Man* (A little grey man) (from Lom); 14, *I Ola-Dalom, i Ola-Kjönn* (In Ola Valley, in Ola Lake) (from Östre Slidre); 15, *Bådnlåt* (Lullaby) (from Lom); 16, *Ho vesle Astrid vor* (Little Astrid) (from Lom); 17, *Bådnlåt* (Lullaby) (from Turtegrö, Sogn); 18, *Jeg går i tusind Tanker* (I wander deep in thought) (from Turtegrö); 19, *Gjendines Bådnlåt* (Gjendine's Lullaby) (from Lom): 56, 62, 64–5, 69, 108, 122, 125.

[1] Anton Seidl's orchestration of Nos. 1–4 was revised by Grieg himself.
[2] For a variant of the same song from Valders, see Works for Vocal Ensemble, Op. 30, No. 5.

OPUS NO.

None. *Tusseslåt* (Procession of Gnomes) (1898): 57.
68.   *Lyriske Stykker* (Lyric Pieces) IX (1898): 1, *Matrosernes Opsang* (Sailor's Song); 2, *Bedstemors Menuet* (Grandmother's Minuet); 3, *For dine Födder* (At your Feet); 4, *Aften på Höjfeldet* (Evening in the Mountains) (arranged for strings, oboe, and horn); 5, *Bådnlåt* (At the Cradle) (arranged for string orchestra); 6, *Valse mélancolique*: 17, 22–4, 53–4, 67.
71.   *Lyriske Stykker* (Lyric Pieces) X (1901): 1, *Der var engang* (Once upon a Time); 2, *Sommeraften* (Summer Evening); 3, *Småtrold* (Puck); 4, *Skovstilhed* (Peace of the Woods); 5, Halling; 6, *Forbi* (Gone); 7, *Efterklang* (Remembrances): 50, 53, 55, 126.
72.   *Slåtter* (Norwegian Peasant Dances) (1902): 1, *Giböens Bruremarsch* (Bridal March); 2, *John Vaestafae's Springdans;* 3, *Bruremarsch* (Bridal March) (from Telemark); 4, *Haugelåt* (Halling from the gnomes' hill); 5, *Prillaren fra Os Praestegjeld* (dance for prillar-horn, from Os); 6, *Gangar* (after 'Myllargutten')[1]; 7, *Rötnamsknut* (Halling from Hallingdal)[2]; 8, *Bruremarsch* (Bridal March) (after 'Myllargutten'); 9, *Nils Rekve's Halling*; 10, *Knut Luråsen's Halling I*; 11, *Knut Luråsen's Halling II*; 12, Springdans (after 'Myllargutten'); 13, *Håvar Giböens Draum ved Oterholtsbrue* (Giböen's Dream. Springdans); 14, *Tussebrure-faere på Vossevangen* (The Goblin's Bridal Procession. Gangar); 15, *Skuldalsbruri* (Skuldal's Bride. Gangar); 16, *Kivlemöyerne* (The girls of Kivledal) (Springdans from Selljord, in Telemark); 17, *Kivlemoyerne* (The Girls of Kivledal) (Gangar): 41, 62, 65–7, 93, 116, 121–2, 125.
73.   *Stemninger* (Moods) (1905): 1, Resignation; 2, Scherzo-Impromptu; 3, *Natligt Ridt* (Night Ride); 4, *Folketone* (Folk Tune) (from Valders)[3]; 5, *Studie*; 6, *Studenternes Serenade* (Students' Serenade); 7, *Lualåt* (Mountaineer's Song): 46, 56, 67–8, 115, 123.
None. *Dansen går* (Wild Dance) (pub. 1908, with *Tusseslåt* and *Hvide Skyer*, see *supra*, as *Tre Klaverstykker*, Three Piano Pieces): 57.

WORKS FOR PIANO DUET

14.   *Deux pièces symphoniques* (1864; arrangement of the slow movement and scherzo of an unpublished Symphony in C minor): 26, 113.
35.   *Firhaendige Danse* (Norwegian Dances) (1881) (arranged for piano solo)[4]: 17, 27, 41, 62, 70, 104, 125.

[1] 'Myllargutten': see p. 93.
[2] Quite different from the song of the same name, from Valders, in the Album for Male Voices (Op. 30, No. 12).
[3] In Lindeman's collection, where it appears as No. 254, it is called *Stutar-Laatt* (Oxen Tune).
[4] No. 1 as based on *Sinklars Marsch* (from Vågå), No. 2 on a halling from Aamot, No. 3 on a traditional halling, No. 4 on a halling from Hallingdal.

Opus No.

37. Valses-Caprices (1883) (arranged for piano solo): No. 1, in C sharp minor; No. 2, in E minor: 50.
64. Symphonic Dances (1898).[1]

WORKS FOR TWO PIANOS

None. Additional parts for second piano to Mozart's Piano Sonatas in F (K.533), C minor (K.457) and the preceding Fantasia (K.475), C major (K.545), and G (K.283) (1877): 115.

51. *Gammel norsk Melodi med variasjoner* (Old Norwegian Melody with variations) (based on *Sjugur å Trollbrura*, Sigurd and the Troll-Bride; cf. No. 4 of *Seks norske fjeldmelodier* under Works for Piano Solo) (1891; orchestrated 1900, with omission of variations 10—4/4, andante—and 12—2/4, allegro marcato—and with cuts in the finale): 17, 27, 61, 119–20, 123.

SOLO SONGS

10. *Fire Romancer* (Chr. Winther) (before 1862): No. 1, *Taksigelse* (Gratitude); 2, *Skovsang* (Woodland Song); 3, *Blomsterne Tale* (The Flowers' Message); 4, *Sang paa Fjeldet* (Song on the Mountain): 74, 76.

2. Four Songs for Alto (1862): No. 1, *Die Müllerin* (The Maid of the Mill) (Chamisso); 2, *Eingehüllt in graue Wolken* (Closely wrapp'd in murky vapour) (Heine); 3, *Ich stand in dunkeln Träumen* (I stood in gloomy musing) (Heine); 4, *Was soll ich sagen?* (What shall I say?) (Chamisso): 74–5.

4. *Seks Digte* (Six Songs) (1863–4): No. 1, *Die Waise* (The Orphan) (Chamisso); 2, *Morgenthau* (Morning Dew) (Chamisso); 3, *Abschied* (Farewell) (Heine); 4, *Jägerlied* (Hunting Song) (Uhland); 5, *Das alte Lied* (The Ancient Song) (Heine); 6, *Wo sind sie hin?* (Whither have they fled?) (Heine): 75.

5. *Hjertets Melodier* (The Heart's Melodies) (H. C. Andersen) (1864): No. 1, *To brune Öjne* (Two Brown Eyes); 2, *Du fatter ej Bölgernes evige Gang* (You know not the waves' eternal motion)[2]; 3, *Jeg elsker Dig* (I love thee)[3]; 4, *Min tanke er et maegtigt Fjeld* (My thought is a mighty mountain): 71, 76–7.

9. *Romancer og Ballader* (Andreas Munch) (Nos. 1–3, 1864; No. 4, 1865): No. 1, *Harpen* (The Harp); 2, *Vuggesang* (Lullaby)[3]; *Solnedgang* (Sunset); 4, *Udfarten* (The Departure): 77, 122.

15, No. 2. *Kjaerlighed* (Love) (H. C. Andersen)[2] (1864): 77.

None. *Dig elsker jeg* (Thee I love) (Casalis) (1865).

---

[1] See note to same composition under Works for Orchestra.
[2] See also Op. 52 (under Works for Piano Solo).
[3] See also Op. 41 (under Works for Piano Solo).

Chronological List of Compositions

Opus No.

None. *Taaren* (The Tear) (H. C. Andersen) (1865).

None. *Soldaten* (The Soldier) (H. C. Andersen) (1865).

None. *Den blonde pige* (The Fair Maiden) (Björnson) (1867).

15, No. 1. *Margretes vuggesang af ' Kongsemnene'* (Margaret's Lullaby from ' The Pretenders ') (Ibsen)[1] (1868): 84.

39, No. 4. *Millom Rosor* (Among the Roses) (Janson) (1869): 86.

18. *Romancer*, Vol. I (Nos. 1–3, 1869; No. 4, 1865): No. 1, *Vandring i Skoven* (Wandering in the Woods) (H. C. Andersen); 2, *Hun er saa hvid* (She is so white)[1] (H. C. Andersen); 3, *En Digters siste Sang* (A Poet's Last Song) (H. C. Andersen); 4, *Efteraars-stormen* (The Autumn Storm) (Chr. Richardt). Vol. II (Nos. 1–4, 1869; No. 5, 1868): No. 1, *Poesien* (Poesy) (H. C. Andersen); 2, *Ungbirken* (The Young Birch Tree) (Moe); 3, *Hytten* (The Hut) (H. C. Andersen); 4, *Rosenknoppen* (The Rosebud) (H. C. Andersen); 5, *Serenade till Welhaven* (Serenade to Welhaven) (Björnson): 19–20, 74, 77–8, 91.

39, No. 1. *Fra Monte Pincio* (From Monte Pincio) (Björnson) (1870)[2]: 22, 76, 81.

None. *Odalisken synger* (The Song of the Odalisque) (Carl Bruun) (1870): 85.

15, No. 3. *Langelandsk Folkemelodi* (Folktune from Langeland) (H. C. Andersen) (1870)

15, No. 4. *Modersorg* (A Mother's Grief) (Richardt)[3] (1870).

21. *Fire Sange* (from *The Fishermaiden*) (Björnson) (Nos. 1–2, 1870; Nos. 3–4, 1872): No. 1, *Det förste möde* (The First Meeting)[3, 4]; 2, *God morgen* (Good Morning); 3, *Jeg giver mit digt til våren* (I give my song to the Spring)[1]; 4, *Tak for dit råd* (Thanks for thy Rede): 74, 80–1.

None. *Prinsessen* (The Princess) (Björnson)[1] (1871): 67, 81, 117.

39, No. 2. *Dulgt kjaerlighed* (Hidden Love) (Björnson) (1872–3): 81.

39, No. 5. *Ved en ung hustrus båre* (At the Bier of a Young Wife) (O. P. Monrad) (1873): 85.

None. *Suk* (Sigh) (Björnson) (1873).

25. *Seks Digte* (Ibsen) (1876): No. 1, *Spillemaend* (Fiddlers) (used as motto of String Quartet, Op. 27); 2. *En svane* (A Swan)[2]; 3, *Stambogsrim* (Verse for an Album); 4, *Med en vandlilje* (With a Waterlily); 5, *Borte* (Departed); 6, *En fuglevise* (A Bird-Song)[5]: 22, 42, 72–4, 76, 82–4.

26. *Fem Digte* (J. Paulsen) (1876): No. 1, *Et håb* (A Hope); 2, *Jeg reiste en deilig sommerkvaeld* (I wandered one lovely summer's

---

[1] See also Op. 41 (under Works for Piano Solo).
[2] Accompaniment orchestrated by the composer in 1894.
[3] See also Op. 52 (under Works for Piano Solo).
[4] See also *Two Melodies*, Op. 53 (under Works for String Orchestra).
[5] Not in Peters Edition.

Opus No.

    eve); 3, *Den aergjerrige* (Ambition)[1]; 4, *Med en primula veris* (With a Primrose); 5, *På skogstien* (On the Woodland Path): 76, 84.

32. *Den Bergtekne* (The Mountain Thrall) (old Norwegian), for baritone, strings and two horns (1878): 17, 22, 86.

33. *Melodier* (A. O. Vinje), Vol. I (No. 5, 1877; Nos. 1–4 and 6, 1880): No. 1, *Guten* (The Youth); 2, *Våren* (Spring)[2]; 3, *Den Sårede* (The Wounded Heart)[2]; 4, *Tyttebaeret* (The Whortleberry); 5, *Langs ei Aa* (Along the River); 6, *Eit Syn* (A Vision). Vol. II (No. 1, 1873; Nos. 2–6, 1880): No. 1. *Gamle Mor* (Old Mother)[3]; 2, *Det Förste* (The First); 3, *Ved Rundarne* (Return to Rundarne); 4, *Et Vennestykke* (A Broken Friendship); 5, *Trudom* (Faith); 6, *Fyremål* (The Goal)[4]: 22, 74, 77, 87–9, 121, 123, 125.

None. *På Hamars Ruiner* (Over Hamar's Ruins) (A. O. Vinje) (1880).

39, No. 3. *Liden höjt deroppe* (High up on the grassy slope) (Jonas Lie) (1885).[1]

39, No. 6. *Hörer jeg sangen klinge* (When I hear that song) (Nordahl Rolfsen, after Heine) (1885): 75.

44. *Fra Fjeld og Fjord* (From Mountain and Fjord) (Holger Drachmann) (1886): No. 1, *Prolog*; 2, *Johanne*; 3, *Ragnhild*; 4, *Ingebjörg*; 5, *Ragna*; 6, *Epilog*: 78.

48. *Seks Sange* (1889): No. 1, *Gruss* (Greeting) (Heine); 2, *Dereinst, Gedanke mein* (Someday, my Thought) (Geibel); 3, *Lauf der Welt* (The Way of the World) (Uhland); 4, *Verschwiegene Nachtigall* (The Discreet Nightingale) (Walther von der Vogelweide); 5, *Zur Rosenzeit* (In the Time of Roses) (Goethe); 6, *Ein Traum* (A Dream) (Bodenstedt): 75–6, 91.

None. *Der Jäger* (The Hunter) (Schultz) (1889)[5]: 76.

None. *Osterlied* (Easter Song) (Böttger) (1889)[5]: 76.

---

[1] Not in Peters Edition.

[2] See also *Elegiac Melodies*, Op. 34 (under Works for String Orchestra).

[3] See also Op. 52 (under Works for Piano Solo).

[4] See also *Two Melodies*, Op. 53 (under Works for String Orchestra).

[5] The conjecture that these two German songs belong to so early a period is a purely personal one. Their style is certainly similar to that of Op. 48, and although their copyright dates are 1908 and 1906 respectively, according to Monrad-Johansen, Grieg's most recent and most exhaustive biographer, the last songs, Op. 69 and 70, were written at Copenhagen in 1900. In 1905, the year usually given for *Der Jäger*, Grieg wrote to Matthison Hansen and, quoting Horneman's gibe at Johan Selmer, said that ' The mountains tremble and there is born—a mouse!' as applying to his own latest work, the piano pieces Op. 73, and that ' my mouse is so small that one needs spectacles to see it '. *Der Jäger* was copyrighted posthumously by Peters in 1908, but appears in Vol. X of the Scandinavian edition of the songs, dated 1905. A possible theory: Kaiser Wilhelm made much of Grieg in 1903–4, even making the orchestra on his yacht learn a whole Grieg programme, which was played when the yacht was anchored in Bergen harbour. The Kaiser entertained him again in Berlin early in 1907, and it is possible that in the enthusiasm of the moment he may have dug out an old manuscript with a German text, furbished it up, dated it 1905, and then forgotten it until Peters found it after his death and published it in 1908. The *Osterlied* does not appear in Vol. X of the Scandinavian edition, but only separately, published by Peters with no date except that of the 1906 copyright. Being a sacred

Opus No.

49. *Seks Digte* (Holger Drachmann) (1889): No. 1, *Saa du Knösen* (Did you see the lad?); 2, *Vug, o Vove* (Rock, O Wave); *Vaer hilset, I Damer* (Greetings to ye Ladies!); 4, *Nu er Aftnen lys og lang* (Now the evening is light and long); 5, *Julesne* (Christmas Snow); 6, *Forårsregn* (Spring Rain): 78–9.

None. *Simpel Sang* (Simple Song) (Holger Drachmann) (1889).

None. *Jeg elsket . . .* (I loved . . .), from the oratorio *Fred* (Peace) (Björnson) (about 1891): 82.

58. *Norge* (Norway) (J. Paulsen) (1894): No. 1, *Hjemkomst* (Homecoming); 2, *Til Norge* (To Norway); 3, *Henrik Wergeland*[1]; 4, *Turisten* (The Tourist); 5, *Udvandreren* (The Emigrant): 84.

59. *Elegiske digte* (Elegiac Poems) (J. Paulsen) (1894): No. 1, *Når jeg vil dö* (When I die); 2, *På Norges nögne fjelde* (On Norway's Bare Mountains) (paraphrase of Heine's ' Ein Fichtenbaum '); 3, *Til En* I (To One); 4, *Til En* II (To One); 5, *Farvel* (Farewell); 6, *Nu hviler du i jorden* (Now that you rest in the earth): 83–5.

60. *Five Songs* (Vilhelm Krag) (1894): No. 1, *Liden Kirsten* (Little Kirsten); 2, *Moderen synger* (The Mother Sings); 3, *Mens jeg venter* (While I wait); 4, *Der skreg en fugl* (There screamed a bird); 5, *Og jeg vil ha mig en hjertenskjaer* (And I will take a sweetheart): 72, 85.

61. *Barnlige Sanger* (Children's Songs) (1894–5): No. 1, *Havet* (Sea-Song) (Nordahl Rolfsen); 2, *Sang til Juletraeet* (Christmas Song) (Johan Krohn); 3, *Lok* (Farmyard Song) (Björnson); 4, *Fiskervise* (Fisher's Song) (Petter Dass); 5, *Kveldsang for Blakken* (Dobbin's Goodnight Song) (Rolfsen); 6, *De norske fjelde* (Song of the Mountains) (Rolfsen); 7, *Faedrelands-Salme* (Fatherland's Psalm) (Runeberg, trs. Rolfsen): 85–6, 126.

67. *Haugtussa Sang-Cyclus* (Arne Garborg) (1896–8): No. 1, *Det syng* (The Singing); 2, *Veslemöy* (Little Maiden); 3, *Blaabaerli* (Bilberry-Slopes); 4, *Möte* (Meeting); 5, *Elsk* (Love); 6, *Killingdans* (Kidlings' Dance); 7, *Vond Dag* (Evil Day); 8, *Ved Gjaetle-Bekken* (At the Brook): 53, 88–91, 121–2.

69. *Fem Digte* (Otto Benzon) (1900): No. 1, *Der gynger en Baad paa Bölge* (A boat is rocking on the waves); 2, *Til min Dreng* (To my Little Son); 3, *Ved Moders Grav* (At Mother's Grave); 4, *Snegl, Snegl, kom ud af dit Hus* (Snail, snail, come out of your house); 5, *Drömme* (Dream): 79.

70. *Fem Digte* (Otto Benzon) (1900): No. 1, *Eros*; 2, *Jeg lever mit Liv i Laengsel* (I live my life in longing); 3, *Lys Nat* (Lucent Night); 4, *Se dig for, naar du vaelger din Vej* (Beware, when you choose your path); 5, *Digtervise* (Poet's Song): 72, 79, 91.

---

song, this may have been written later in Germany or at some other time nearer the Psalms for mixed choir, Op. 74, which date from 1906; but that would not square with Johansen's definite statement that no songs were written after 1900.—A. D.

[1] Accompaniment orchestrated by composer in 1894.

Opus No.

None. *Ave Maris Stella* (arranged for S.A.T.B. chorus, a cappella, 1899): 109.

None. *Julens Vuggesang* (Christmas Lullaby) (Langsted) (1900): 80.

MELODRAMA

42. *Bergljot* (Björnson), for declamation and piano (1871; orchestrated 1885): 17, 23, 96–7.

DRAMATIC WORKS

22. Incidental music to Björnson's *Sigurd Jorsalfar* (Sigurd the Crusader) (1872): 1, *Borghilds Dröm* (Borghild's Dream) (intermezzo in Act I); 2, March, *Ved Mandjaevningen* (The Matching Game) (introduction to Act II) (based on Gavotte for violin and piano; see under Chamber Music); 3, *Kvad: Norrönafolket* (The Northland Folk) (end of Act II); 4, *Hyldnings Marsch* (Homage March) (Act III); 5, *Konge Kvadet* (The Song of the Kings) (end of Act III).[1] See also Op. 56, under Orchestral Works: 23–4, 40, 94–5, 107.

23. Incidental music to Ibsen's *Peer Gynt* (1874–5; re-orchestrated 1886). (For details see p. 104; see also Op. 46 and 55 under Orchestral Works, and Op. 47, No. 4, and Op. 52, No. 4, under Works for Piano Solo): 18, 23–4, 49, 55, 63, 69, 74, 82, 86, 100–5, 116–7, 120–1, 124–5.

50. Fragment of opera, *Olav Trygvason* (Björnson) (1873; orchestrated 1889 as *Scenes from ' Olav Trygvason '*) (Prayer and Temple Dance arranged for piano solo): 97–101, 103, 108.

Sketches for opera *Arnljot Gjelline* (Björnson) (1872).

WORKS FOR CHORUS AND ORCHESTRA

None. Cantata for the Unveiling of the Christie Monument, Bergen, for chorus and orchestra (1868).

20. *Foran Sydens Kloster* (At a Southern Convent Gate) (from Björnson's *Arnljot Gjelline*) for soprano and contralto soli, S.S.A.A. chorus and orchestra (1871): 94, 107.

22. Two Songs from *Sigurd Jorsalfar* (see footnote under Dramatic Works).

31. *Landkjaenning* (Recognition of Land) (Björnson), for baritone solo, T.T.B.B. chorus, orchestra and organ *ad lib.* (1872; drastically revised 1881): 96, 108.

Sketches for the oratorio *Fred* (Peace) (Björnson) (1891); see under Solo songs.

SMALLER WORKS FOR VOCAL ENSEMBLE

None. *Rückblick*, for chorus and piano (1863).

None. *Björnskytten* (The Bear Hunt) (Jörgen Moe), for T.T.B.B. (1867).

[1] Nos. 3 and 5 afterwards published in Germany as ' Two Songs from *Sigurd Jorsalfar*, Op. 22, Nos. 1 and 2 '.

Opus No.

None. *Aftenstemning* (Evening Mood) (Jörgen Moe), for T.T.B.B. (1867).

None. *Den norske sjömand* (The Norwegian Sailor) (Björnson) for male voices (1868).

None. Cantata for the 25th Anniversary of Hals Brothers' Piano Factory, Christiania (Björnson).

30. *Album for Mandssang (frit efter norske folkeviser)* (Album for Male Voices: free arrangements of Norwegian folk-tunes) 1877–8). No. 1, *Jeg lagde mig så sildig* (I laid me down so late) (from Vaage) (baritone solo and T.T.B.B.); 2, *Bådn-Låt* (Children's Song) (humoreske for two tenors and baritone soli and T.T.B.B.) (from Valders); 3, *Torö liti* (Little Torö) (for baritone solo and T.T.B.B.); 4, Halling (for baritone solo and T.T.B.B.); 5, *Dae ae den störste Dårlehet* (It is the greatest folly) (from Valders)[1] (for baritone solo and T.T.B.B.); 6, *Går e ut ein Kveld* (If I go out in the evening) (springdans for baritone solo and T.T.B.B.); 7, *Han Ole* (Young Ole) (from Valders) (for baritone solo and T.T.B.B.); 8, Halling (for tenor solo and T.T.B.B.); 9, *Deiligste blandt kvinder* (Fairest of women) (from Raulandstrand) (for T.T., baritone, B.B. soli or chorus); 10, *Den store, hvide Flok* (The great, white Host) (from Hittersdal) (for baritone solo and T.T.B.B.); 11, *Fantegutten* (The Gypsy Lad) (for T.T., baritone, B.B. soli or baritone and small chorus); 12, *Rötnams Knut* (from Valders) (for T.T.B.B. soli or chorus): 41, 107–8, 121.

None. *Sangerhilsen (Lad os hvirvle velkomstsangen)* (A Greeting from Singers: Let us sing a song of welcome) (Sigvald Skavlan) (1883).

None. *Holberg-Kantate* (Nordahl Rolfsen) (for baritone solo and T.T.B.B.) (1884).

None. Cantata for the Unveiling of the Kjerulf Statue in Christiania.

None. Song for Norway's Constitution Day, for male voices (1893).

74. Four Psalms (based freely on old Norwegian psalm-tunes) (1906) No. 1, *Hvad est du dog skjön* (How fair is Thy face) (for S.A.T.B.); 2, *Guds Sön har gjort mig fri* (God's Son hath set me free) (for baritone solo and S.A.T.B.); 3, *Jesus Kristus er opfaren* (Jesus Christ our Lord is risen) (for S.A.T.B.); 4, *I Himmelen* (In Heaven above) (for baritone solo and S.A.T.B.): 65, 106, 109, 121, 125.

None. *Kristiansernes Sangerhilsen (Nu Pintsens Klokker ringer)* (Greeting from Christiania's Singers) (Jonas Lie) (for baritone solo and T.T.B.B.).

None. *Ved Welhaven's Båre (Stille nu!)* (By Welhaven's Grave) (Jörgen Moe).

[1] For a variant of the same song from Söndmöre, see Works for Piano Solo, Op. 66, No. 2.

MUSICAL EXAMPLES

Ex. 1

Grieg

Ex.2 contd.

etc.

etc.

Ex.3

Ex.4

Grieg

4

A
Solo Pianist's entry

Ex.6

Grieg

Ex.7

etc.

Picc.

Fl.

Ob.

Cl. in B♭

Bsn.

Hns. in F

Trpts. in F

Trbs. I
II

B. Trb.

Tuba

Vln. I

Vln. II

Vlas.

Celli.

Bass

etc.

Grieg

6

Ex. 8

Grieg

Ex. 9

Grieg

Ex. 10

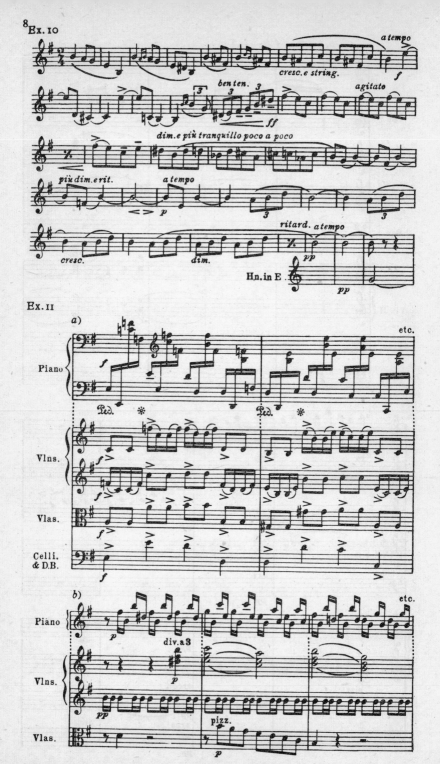

Ex. 11

Grieg

Ex.12

Cello continues with melody, with basses,
against strings, 2 clarinets, and 3 horns
(*pp*, off the beat).

Grieg

Ex. 13

Tempo di Mazurka

+Die Triller ohne Nachschlag

Ex. 14

Grieg

Ex. 15

Ex. 16

Grieg

Ex. 17

Ex. 18

Grieg

Ex. 19

Grieg

Grieg

Ex. 26

Grieg

Grieg

Ex.31

Ex.32

Ex.33

Grieg

Grieg

Ex. 38

Ex. 39

Grieg

Ex.40

Grieg

Ex.42

Ex.43

Ex.44 Tranquillo

Ex.45

Ex.46

Ex.47

Grieg

Ex. 48

Ex. 49

Ex. 50

Grieg

Ex.51

Ex.52

Grieg

Ex.53

Ex.54

Grieg

Ex.58
Andante tranquillo

p ... etc.

Ex.59
a)

b)

pp

Ex.60
(From No.6) ♩. = 76

Violin

Grieg's
arrangement

marcato

ff

p

cresc. molto

Grieg

28

Ex.61

Grieg

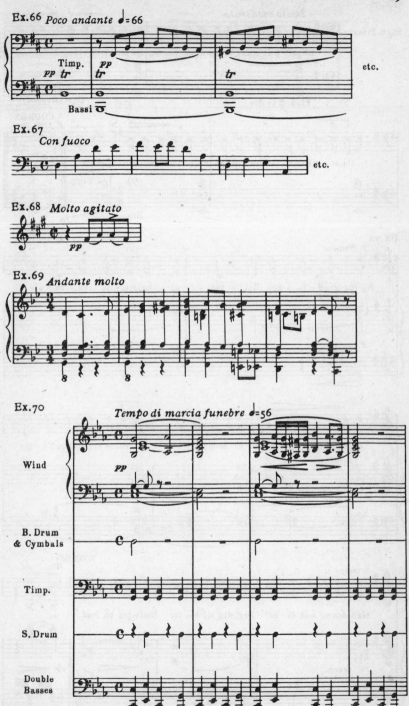

Ex.66 *Poco andante* ♩=66

Timp.

pp *tr*

Bassi

etc.

Ex.67

Con fuoco

etc.

Ex.68 *Molto agitato*

pp

Ex.69 *Andante molto*

Ex.70

Tempo di marcia funebre ♩=56

Wind

pp

B. Drum
& Cymbals

Timp.

S. Drum

Double
Basses

Grieg

Ex. 71

Grieg

Ex. 77

Ex. 78

Ex. 79

Ex. 80

Ex. 81

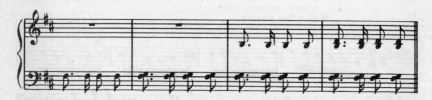

Grieg

Ex.82 *Lentamente*

Jeg lag - de mig så sil - dig alt sent _ om en

kveld, Jeg vids - te in - gen kvi - de til at ha - ve;

Ex.83

Ex. 84

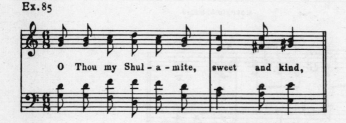

Ex.85

O Thou my Shul - a - mite, sweet and kind,

Ex.86

Yea fair.

Grieg

34

Ex. 87

Not too slowly

I sko - gen små - gut - ten gik da - gen lang, gik

da - gen lang, der hav - de han hørt slig en un - der - lig sang,

un - der - lig sang.

marcato il basso

Ex. 88

a) *Allegretto tranquillamente*

GRIEG. BÅDNLÅT. Op. 68. No. 5

Grieg

Ex.88 *Allegro*
b)

COUPERIN. 23me Ordre

Ex.89 *Lento*

Ex.90

Men skyg - ged   gjor_ de det mør - ke   fjeld,   Og   du, du

fandt ik - ke ve -   jen.   p (*Humming to herself*)

dim. e rit.

mf   pp

rit.

pp poco rit.

Grieg

Ex. 91   *Moderato*   HALLING Arr. LINDEMAN

Ex. 92

Ex. 93

Vivace

Nei sjå, kor det blå - ner her! No må me ro - a oss,

Ky - ra! Å nei, sli - ke fi - ne Boer, Og dei, som det ber - re kry - ra!

Grieg

Grieg

Ex. 97 (From Op. 72. No. 3)

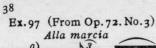

Alla marcia

a)

(From Op. 72. No. 2)

b) *Allegro moderato*

Ex. 98

Allegretto espressivo

Grieg

Ex. 99
Andante espressivo

End – nu en Gang så jeg I__ sen, den blå fra Lan – det at fly – de.

Ex. 100
a) *Allegretto semplice*

GRIEG Op. 73. No. 7

etc.

b) *Lento moderato*

WAGNER. Tristan and Isolde. III. i.

etc.

Ex. 101
Allegro con moto

con Pedale

rubato

Grieg

40

Ex. 102

Ex. 103

Ex. 104

Grieg